Red Letter Days

other books by the same author:

✧ POEMS FOR RED LETTER DAYS ✧ ONE THOUSAND
POEMS FOR CHILDREN ✧ THIRTEEN GHOSTLY YARNS ✧
HEIGH-HO FOR HALLOWEEN ✧ CHRISTMAS EVERYWHERE

in collaboration with Janette Woolsey:

✧ IT'S TIME FOR CHRISTMAS ✧ IT'S TIME FOR EASTER
✧ IT'S TIME FOR THANKSGIVING ✧ IT'S TIME FOR
BROTHERHOOD ✧ IT'S TIME FOR STORY HOUR ✧ IT'S
TIME TO GIVE A PLAY ✧ NEW PLAYS FOR RED LETTER
DAYS

Red Letter Days

A BOOK OF HOLIDAY CUSTOMS

Elizabeth Hough Sechrist

Illustrations by Elsie Jane McCorkell

REVISED EDITION

Macrae Smith Company
PHILADELPHIA

Third Printing

Library of Congress Catalog Card Number 65-16332
Manufactured in the United States of America

6509

ACKNOWLEDGMENTS

The author wishes to thank Houghton, Mifflin Company for permission to quote from the poem, "Decoration Day," by Henry Wadsworth Longfellow; the Curtis Publishing Company for permission to quote from "The Mother of Mother's Day" by Ann Hark, published in *The Country Gentleman;* the United States Department of Agriculture for permission to use material from their publications *Arbor Day* and *Famous Trees;* Professor Walter F. Rothé, President of the Universal Calendar Society, Inc., for information on the proposed Universal Calendar; Miss Elisabeth Achelis, former President of the World Calendar Association for her advice; Mr. and Mrs. Timothy Wilson of Midlothian, Scotland, for information about Scottish holiday customs; Mrs. Anne Babbitt Kerr for material on holidays in the South; and lastly, the publishers of the hundreds of books, pamphlets and periodicals to which she is indebted.

TO MY SISTER

Clare Hough Babbitt

WITH MY DEVOTION

Foreword to the New Edition

For some years we have been aware of the need for a revision of *Red Letter Days*. In the twenty-five years that have passed since it was first published, many changes have taken place in our ever-changing world. Although any history of our nation's holidays is necessarily based on tradition and custom, it remains a fact that much of what was contemporary a quarter of a century ago is now out of date. This is particularly true of our younger holidays. In 1939, one wrote of *the* World War, and the League of Nations, and spoke hopefully of peace for the world. Today we are forced to admit that wars did not cease after the Treaty of Versailles. We look back and see the development of the atom bomb, the split ideologies of world powers, the growing threat of Communism in our hemisphere. But also there are the bright spots of the past twenty-five years, so that when we write about Veterans Day (it used to be Armistice Day) we can talk about the United Nations; and in the discussion of Pan-American Day we are able to present the hopeful plans of the OAS and the Alliance for Progress. These are only a few of the changes relating to our holidays today.

While we observe new and significant celebrations, it is good to know that we also continue to love the old customs, for though we subscribe to new ways we are still tied irrevocably to the old.

E.H.S.

Contents

CONTENTS

Preface

Holidays have been observed by all races and classes since ancient times. Indeed, it is not hard to imagine the cavemen of a prehistoric age celebrating some particularly successful hunting or fishing expedition by proclaiming a holiday! The impulse to make a momentous occasion of the anniversary of an important event seems almost instinctive to civilized man, and from historic records we know that anniversaries and red-letter days of all kinds have given us the holidays we celebrate today.

Many of our American holidays are comparatively young, but even a nation as new as our own is rich in tradition. Thanksgiving inherited from the Pilgrim Fathers, Independence Day commemorating the birth of our country, Columbus Day, Constitution Day, Flag Day—all are identified with our early history. Armistice Day and Pan-American Day link us with other nations, while Christmas, Easter, and New Year's we share with mankind the world over. Days like St. Patrick's Day, St. Valentine's Day, May Day and Halloween, though not legal holidays, have a definite place on our calendar because they have become so enriched by centuries of custom that their observance has never ceased.

It is impossible to study the history of our holidays without being conscious of the history and growth of the peoples who observed them. In most parts of the world certain days are observed which may have a significance to one country alone, holidays that have developed with the nation. In this book it did not seem necessary to include any except those that were similar to or comparable with some holiday of our own. However, many of our holidays inherited from the Old World are colored with ancient customs reflecting the manners and customs of some civilization of the past—the ancient Romans, the Celts of Britain, the Medieval English, or the peasants of Ireland, Scotland and Wales, as well as our own Colonial ancestors. When we observe these old holidays today we are keeping alive in the present the traditions of the past, for they have a foothold so firmly rooted that modern ways cannot push them completely from the calendar. Let us hope that it will be a long, long time before these colorful customs vanish. Long may they thrive!

ELIZABETH HOUGH SECHRIST

Red Letter Days

New Year's Day

JANUARY I

Time, moving along unceasingly, waits for no man, linking the years together in an endless chain. When New Year's Eve comes and the clock strikes the last hour of the last day of the old year, we feel ourselves being carried along on the tide of time, looking ahead hopefully to the new year that lies before us. Another January 1, another beginning!

The new year has not always begun on January 1. In Ancient Egypt, thousands of years ago, the year began at the time of the overflowing of the River Nile, which occurred about the middle of June. The early Romans began their year in March, just as the Ancient Babylonians had done long before them, but it was a famous Roman who changed the date of New Year's to January 1. The Julian Calendar, Julius Cæsar's new method of reckoning time, was a forerunner of our own. In Anglo-Saxon England the twenty-first of December was New Year's Day until William the Conqueror changed it to January 1. England was to know other New Year's Days, however, for it later observed March 25, along with other nations of the world. In 1752 England adopted the Gregorian Calendar and January 1 again, this time permanently, as New Year's.

The Ancient Romans named the first month of their year January in honor of Janus. He was the god of two faces and could look backward and forward. On New Year's Day the Romans looked back, in reviewing the events of the year, and forward to the new year ahead.

The Romans have been given credit for the origin of giving gifts at New Year's, a custom practiced in some countries today. It is said that Augustus Cæsar claimed to have had a vision in which he saw himself receiving gifts from the Senate and the people on the Kalends of January.

When the Romans invaded England several hundred years later, they brought this custom with them. In England, at the time of Queen Elizabeth I, there was a special ceremony at Court for exchanging presents. Historians claim that practically all of Elizabeth's wardrobe and jewelry came to her as New Year's gifts. Among other gifts, she acquired a collection of hundreds of pairs of embroidered and bejeweled gloves. It was about this time that the term

18

"pin money" originated. After the invention of this useful article, when money was given to the ladies at New Year's it was called pin money because they were so intrigued with pins that some would, in all probability, be the object of their spending.

An important feature of New Year's Day in early England was the Wassail Bowl. A drink called *lamb's wool* was carefully blended in the large Wassail Bowl and then handed around to every member of the gathering, each person wishing the other "Wæs hæil!"—"Be thou well!" Also made especially for New Year's consumption were the popular god cakes, cut into triangles of all sizes and filled with mincemeat filling.

In the olden days New Year's was considered a good time to foretell the future, to look ahead into the year just beginning. One custom was known as "dipping." The family Bible was read by the master of the house. He opened the book with eyes closed, and the passage found by his finger indicated the fortune of his house for the ensuing year. The text was read solemnly and interpreted by the family as a prognostication of the luck, good or ill, that would befall.

Probably the most widespread of all New Year's superstitions and the one that was taken most seriously was that concerning the "first-footer!" The type of person who first set foot in the house on the first day of the year was considered extremely important. For instance, it was very bad luck for a woman to enter one's house first on New Year's Day, and unlucky for the first-footer to be a light-haired man. Among others considered unlucky were gravediggers, persons who walked with their toes turned in, those whose eyebrows met, and men with red or blond hair! In many villages, in order to avoid any catastrophe such an occurrence might bring upon an innocent household, a dark-haired man was chosen as a first-footer and his job was to go from house to house where he would be first to enter, preserving the good fortune of the house. If everybody who entered on the first day of the year carried food into the house, that was considered good luck. Among the working classes there was such a fear of starvation that a peculiar ceremony was practiced in many homes to ward off this stark enemy! "Breaking the cake," it was called. A special New Year's cake was dashed with much force against the door; then everybody rushed to pick up a piece and eat it, praying meanwhile that neither hunger nor want should enter that house. It was considered very bad luck to throw anything out on this day, even if it were ashes or a bit of rubbish. Superstitious people were filled with untold dread if, by accident or forgetfulness, someone carried from the house a light or a candle, for they believed that this meant death to a member of that household before the year was past.

In Scotland, where New Year's Day is known as Hogmanay, it is still the custom to go "first-footing" after midnight on Hogmanay Eve. A guest who puts a first-foot over the threshold is invited in to drink a toast. By tradition he must take his hosts a bottle of spirits and a piece of coal.

In return he will receive a "black bun"—a rich fruit cake—or that Scottish delicacy, shortbread.

"Burning out the old year" by building huge bonfires to which everybody added some fuel was a popular custom all over Great Britain. In recent years, however, except in some remote places, the practice is dying out. In Biggar, a town in Lanarkshire, Scotland, the ancient custom is still religiously observed by the townspeople. The tradition is that if the ritual is omitted for a single time the charm must be considered broken and the custom will have ceased. At ten o'clock a huge fire is built and in the ashes "herring and 'tatties [potatoes]" are baked for the consumption of all participating in the fun. At midnight the new year is ushered in with the lusty singing of *Auld Lang Syne,* written by their own Bobby Burns. Then the people go to their homes, except for a few who remain to keep the fires burning through the night.

In Sussex, England, there is an old custom of throwing apples, oranges, and nuts out the window to be scrambled for by the fishermen of the town. A quaint custom said to have persisted from the time of the Druids is practiced in Northumberland; twenty-four men dressed in old-time costumes march around the town from eleven thirty until midnight with pans of blazing tar on their heads. The children of Northumberland beg for gifts of coins on New Year's Day, saying, "Old Year out, New Year in, please give us a New Year's gift."

In Scotland, the children used to go in a procession from

house to house on Hogmanay Eve asking for oat bread and cheese.

> *Get up, good wife, and shake your feathers,*
> *And dinna think that we are beggars;*
> *For we are bairns come out to play,*
> *Get up and gie's our Hogmanay.*

The Monday after New Year's, known as Handsel Monday, is Boxing Day in Scotland. "Handsel" is the old English word for money. This is also the day of a feast, and on every table there is sure to be found plenty of the special cakes that are made by the good housewives of Scotland—oaten cakes and wheat cakes, all decorated, many of them bearing the greeting "A merrie auld Yule!"

In France, as in Scotland, New Year's is the important holiday of the year when gifts are exchanged. All day the doorbells ring, for besides those who leave packages there are the tradesmen who come to the door and wish the people of the house *"Bonne année!"* and receive, in turn, gifts of money. There is a most joyous atmosphere among the people of this happy nation at the holiday season, an abundance of good will with feasting, drinking each other's health, and much gaiety. New Year's gifts are proudly displayed for the many callers who come and go throughout the day. And yet the *Jour de l'an* has its serious side, too. New Year's Eve is also the Vigil of St. Sylvester, and the churches are generally crowded, while in some of the remote country places there is a quaint custom, on this Eve of Sylvester, of driving the cattle to the door of the church, where the priest says Mass for their protection for the year to follow. Another custom in France is the visiting of graves by the families of the departed ones, since this day is thought to be a good time to remember the dead as well as the living.

New Year's Eve in Switzerland is also celebrated as Sylvester Day. On that day the children call the lazy one of the family, or the one who is last out of bed, a "Sylvester!"

The Armenians' New Year is much like our Christmas. There it is customary for friends of the family to lower a basket of gifts down the chimney!

St. Basil's Day is celebrated in Greece on January 1 in honor of St. Basil, who was Bishop of Cæsarea in the fourth century. On that day the carolers go about singing songs and carrying a miniature "St. Basil's ship" to represent the boat on which the Saint sailed from Cæsarea. The Greeks also have Basil-cakes that everyone eats on New Year's— round, flat, savory morsels. The baking of these cakes is a traditional ceremony, even the wealthiest of the Greek women performing this task with their own hands and donning their very best clothes and jewelry for the occasion. The master of the house makes the sign of the cross as he cuts the cake. Happy is that member of the family who finds the small silver coin that has been placed therein, for great good luck is believed in store for the one whose cake contains it!

Rumania is another country that combines the St. Basil celebration with the New Year's. On New Year's Eve young people go about from house to house, ringing bells, crack-ing whips, and singing songs of New Year's greetings. On the next day these greetings are continued and the people throw corn at each other for good luck.

To the people of the Far East the first day of the New Year is very important indeed. Japanese bells ring out 108 times, as a reminder of the 108 commandments of Buddha, at midnight in the Buddhist temples, to usher in the New Year. The holiday was formerly celebrated for two weeks, but now that the Gregorian Calendar has been adopted by the Japanese nation, the longer celebration is not so uni-versally observed. However, many of the ancient customs still prevail. One of these is the practice of scattering parched beans to the four corners of the house so that the devils will be driven from the place and good luck will enter. Then a straw rope is tied across the door to keep out all evil. The housewives will have been very busy getting ready for the holiday. The house is cleaned from top to bottom and the broom tied up so that no sweeping can be done on New Year's Day, for this might frighten away the good spirits! Another task of the Japanese housewife is to secure sacred coals from the temple with which to start her fire to cook the New Year's dinner. Certain symbolic dishes are served on specific days of the New Year festival. For instance, on the third day, small hard rice cakes—*mochi*—are eaten with a special good-luck tea and preserved plums. The plum denotes old age, the significance being that those who eat the plum will be blessed with long life. On the

24

seventh day all partake of the "gruel of the seven herbs" to rid the mind and body of evil during the year to come.

After having used the lunar calendar for more than four thousand years, the Chinese as well as the Japanese have begun to observe January 1 as New Year's, showing the occidental influence in the East. New Year's in China has always been a time of friendship and good will. Celebrations are in the home, where the family sit at a round table so that the family circle will be, and remain, unbroken. Many of the old Chinese customs are still observed by some, though many of the modern Chinese have dropped the significant and meaningful customs of their forefathers. Making calls on New Year's Day is thought to have originated with the Chinese, a custom that is now observed in many lands. The people of China and Japan can call on their friends with a clear conscience, for in those countries they start the new year with a clean slate. They pay *all* debts before the stroke of midnight on the last day of the year!

Another custom common to China and Japan is that of adding a year to one's age on New Year's Day! Besides being the birthday of the year, it is the birthday of every person—man, woman, or child—in the land.

Eating seven dinners on the last day of the year is a ritual with the people of Mongolia and an enjoyable one for these hardy people, who ordinarily eat once a day. They call New Year's Day the "First of the White Month."

When one observes the year's birthday in India depends upon one's religion, although many Indians do celebrate

January 1. A unique custom there is that of handing friends a lime or lemon on New Year's Day. Consequently, the fruit markets do an immense business the week preceding the holiday. Many people keep a basket beside their door which piles high with the fruit before the day is over. Those of the same caste present each other with flowers and wreaths to be worn around the neck.

March 21 is New Year's Day for the people of Iran, but they celebrate it for two full weeks. It is deemed most important for the homes to be spick and span and for everybody to have new clothes to wear on the holiday. To ensure happiness for all the family, seven foods beginning with the letter "s" are included in the New Year's dinner. The Iranians present each other with eggs, symbol of the beginning of life.

To the Jewish people the New Year is known as the Head of the Year, the day as *Rosh Hashana*. On that day every Jew is called to account for all his deeds throughout the year—those who deserve it, to have their names written in the Book of Life; those who are entirely discreditable, to be eternally condemned. But those who are not entirely on the wrong path may have nine days of grace in which to perform good deeds. This period of time is up at Yom Kippur, the Day of Atonement. A twenty-four–hour fast precedes Yom Kippur, ending at sunset when a trumpet sounds, signifying the closing of the Book of Life. Candles are burned during this time of fast in the homes of every

Orthodox Jew, while many spend the hours at prayer in the synagogue.

When compared with customs of other countries throughout the world, our New Year's Day here in America seems to be one of events rather than of tradition. A huge parade, a nationally heralded football game, a rose festival—these and many other events are established customs in this country. Until recent years one of these was the historic President's Reception at the White House, an annual event that started the first year America had a President. New Year's calls were almost unheard of in colonial times anywhere except in New York City, and when George Washington went to New York as President of the new republic, he was pleasantly surprised at the custom. On that first New Year's Day the President and Mrs. Washington started the custom that was kept up until 1934.

It used to be the practice in New York City, especially during the "Gay Nineties," when much entertaining was done, for the newspapers to publish a list of the people in the city who would receive callers on New Year's Day. The names filled several columns. Making calls on the first day of the new year, even in New York, has lost its popularity, but the custom dies hard and many people still "go the rounds."

Carnivals are very popular in the South, where the weather is warm and the people are carnival-minded. But the southerners are not the only ones who have New Year's carnivals and parades. One of the most famous parades in the country is that held by the mummers in Philadelphia. The origin of this parade goes back to colonial times when Swedish settlers used to observe New Year's by masquerading and going about town, gay and hilarious, to celebrate the new year in what they considered an appropriate manner. These bands of mummers were finally organized in 1876, and in 1901 they were given their first permits to parade. The members of the organization, consisting of many different clubs throughout the city, compete for prizes. The most spectacular costumes in the parade are worn by the presidents of the clubs—costumes that are often almost grotesque in their ornateness and size. Some of them weigh so much that it is a problem for the wearer to walk the long miles of city streets, lined with hundreds of thousands of spectators. Gaily costumed string bands provide lilting music for the occasion.

The Mummers' Parade in Philadelphia is usually made through icy streets on a typical Eastern-seaboard winter day, while on the same day in Pasadena, California, another parade is in progress featuring sunshine and blossoms! This is the Tournament of Roses, a magnificent display of roses and other flowers. Floats are covered with millions of them, in the forms of boats and ships and airplanes and houses and gardens. The Pasadena Tournament of Roses Association has been producing these beautiful parades since 1866.

The Rose Bowl in Pasadena on New Year's Day is the center of interest for sport fans because of the intercollegiate football game played there between the leading team of the Western Conference and one chosen from the Big Ten of the Midwest.

The Chinatowns of several United States cities celebrate the Chinese New Year, which comes late in January. Spectacular parades, usually featuring the Lion Dance, are the main feature of the celebration. The parade in San Francisco attracts great crowds of people. In New York, grown-ups and children alike throw firecrackers as the big "good luck" dragons pass.

Traditional foods that are eaten on New Year's Day in

some sections of the states were introduced by the early colonists. For example, the popular custom all through the South of ensuring good luck by eating black-eyed peas on this day probably was brought from their mother country by the French settlers.

The warm, sunny climate of Mexico makes it a country of fairs, carnivals, and festivals. The Mexicans love music, dancing, and the sunny outdoors, and all these can be had in plenty at a carnival. New Year's Day finds the people of Mexico enjoying fairs all over the land, with rodeos, bull-fights and cockfights, plays and outdoor pageants, parades and races. It is a holiday happily anticipated.

"This is the year that for you waits," the poet says. And, conversely, we wait for the new year! People all over the world are waiting for that last, long minute of the old year to tick out, for the last grain of sand in the hourglass to fall, for the last dying breath of the year that is done. Then at last that very second has arrived: it is twelve o'clock, and the New Year stands on the threshold, peering in at us. Clocks in village, town, and city are striking the hour while church bells are pealing, whistles in the cities and on the ships in the harbor are blowing, and everywhere—at every corner and in every place where there are people—horns are tooted and tin pans beat merrily. Somewhere off in the distance a cannon booms. The New Year has been shot in, and men, women, and children from every walk of life shout gladly to each other, "Happy New Year!"

Lincoln's Birthday

Every school child knows the story of Abraham Lincoln's life, from his birth in the crudely built log cabin down to his last years in the White House in Washington; of his careers as storekeeper, lawyer, congressman, and President; and of his tragic death at the close of the war. There is so much in the life of Lincoln to kindle inspiration in the hearts of young Americans that none can afford to miss the details of it. Of all the biographies of great Americans, his is probably the most popular with young and old alike.

The memory of him as emancipator of a race, martyr to a great cause, and believer in the right is cherished by every true American. There are many portraits and statues of

Lincoln, so that his likeness is familiar to all, but Abraham Lincoln described his appearance in a short biography of himself with these words: "If any personal description of me is thought desirable, it may be said I am in height six feet four inches, nearly; lean in flesh, weighing, on an average, one hundred and eighty pounds; dark complexion, with coarse black hair and gray eyes—no other marks or brands recollected." Lincoln was by nature a retiring man, modest and humble. His shy manner was sometimes mistaken for rudeness while he lived, but all who really knew the man knew his great, kind heart, incapable of rudeness. Lincoln was never known to give deliberate offense to anyone.

As is so often the case with great personages, Lincoln's true worth, his extreme brilliance and clearsightedness as a statesman, were not truly appreciated until after his death. Since then many biographies have been written about him, and Lincoln's own writings have become world-famous. Abe the boy, Lincoln the man, Lincoln the statesman and President, have come alive in the words and by the pen of those who knew him or have made exhaustive studies of his life.

Everything of interest because of its connection with Abraham Lincoln has become touched with tradition and monetary value. One of the most outstanding collections of Lincolniana was the Osborn H. Oldroyd Collection. Mr. Oldroyd through his entire lifetime collected objects that had to do with the life of Lincoln. The collection was

housed in a red-brick building, an old boardinghouse, across the street from the Ford Theatre, where Lincoln was fatally shot. In 1926, when Mr. Oldroyd was an old man, he presented his precious collection to the Federal government. Each piece of the many hundreds of objects in the collection was dear to this old collector's heart because of its association with his hero.

Another notable contribution to Lincolniana is that given to the Library of Congress in Washington by the President's son, Robert Todd Lincoln. Mr. Lincoln began depositing a large collection of letters, manuscripts, and papers belonging to his father in the Library of Congress in 1919. When in 1922 he completed the collection, he presented it to the Library of Congress with a deed providing that "all of said letters, manuscripts, documents and other papers shall be placed in a sealed vault or compartment and carefully preserved from official or public inspection or private view until the expiration of twenty-one years from the date of my death."

The collection of more than eighteen thousand items was released precisely at 12:01 A.M. on July 26, 1947, in the presence of a group of professors, writers, and photographers. The author of *The Lincoln Papers,* David C. Mearns, calls them "not only Lincoln's thoughts and problems, but the inner history of the nation in a time of crisis."

Letters from Lincoln have been used in great number by two of his greatest biographers, John G. Nicolay, private secretary to President Lincoln, and his Secretary of State, John Hay.

Aside from books that have told Lincoln's story, and many portraits of the tall, strong, homely character, there are shrines to Lincoln throughout the nation that are further proof of his endearment to the hearts of his countrymen. Probably the most beautiful of all these is the Lincoln Memorial erected in the nation's capital. Dedicated in 1922, it was built at a cost of three million dollars. The remarkably fine statue of Lincoln seated in a chair, done by the sculptor Daniel Chester French, is the center of the memorial.

Because of their importance as noted objects of sculpture in America, and because they contribute much to the memory of Lincoln, some of his shrines are listed below:

☆ Lincoln's tomb at Springfield, Illinois

☆ Memorial near his birthplace at
   Hodgenville, Kentucky

☆ St. Gaudens's "Seated Lincoln" at Grant Park,
   Chicago, Illinois

☆ St. Gaudens's "Lincoln Standing,"
   Westminster, London

☆ George Gray Bernard statue—original in
   Cincinnati, Ohio, with copies in Manchester,
   England, and Louisville, Kentucky

☆ Gutzon Borglum's amazing figure of Lincoln
   at Newark, New Jersey, seated on a bench,
   his hat beside him—so lifelike that children
   often believe it is real

The Lincoln Center for the Performing Arts, in New York City, is planned as a complex of six buildings. The first, Philharmonic Hall, was completed and dedicated in September, 1962. Others have been opened since then.

The small village in Illinois where Lincoln served as storekeeper and courted Ann Rutledge was recreated by William Randolph Hearst in 1918 at the New Salem State Park and presented to the State of Illinois. In 1931 Nancy Hanks's cabin was dedicated at Harrodsburg, Kentucky, in memory of the time 125 years before when she and Thomas Lincoln were married and made the little log cabin their home in the first white settlement west of the Allegheny Mountains.

Probably the first institution to be named for Abraham Lincoln was the Lincoln Memorial University at Harrogate, Tennessee. It was founded in 1863 at the instigation of Lincoln. Another college taking his name was Lincoln University in Missouri for the training of Negroes. It was started in 1866 with a fund of five thousand dollars raised by the Sixty-second Colored Infantry.

One of the most-traveled highways in the world is the Lincoln Highway. Stretching across the United States from the Atlantic to the Pacific, from New York to San Francisco, it is 3,384 miles long.

An outstanding memorial to Lincoln is Gutzon Borglum's tremendous piece of sculpture at the Mt. Rushmore National Memorial in South Dakota. The bust of Lincoln, far to the right, appears beside carved portraits of George Washington, Thomas Jefferson, and Theodore Roosevelt. The Lincoln head was completed in 1937 and unveiled on September 17 of that year. The stupendous sculpturing feat, conceived by Doane Robinson in 1924, is said to be the greatest piece of work of its kind since the era of the ancient Egyptians. The four busts of Washington, Jefferson, Lincoln, and Roosevelt were built to the gigantic proportions of men 465 feet tall. A profile of an Indian, Chief Crazy Horse, is now being added to the group. The motive behind this immense monument has been "to perpetuate the founding, the expansion, the preservation, and the unification of the United States."

Lincoln's Birthday was first observed ten months after his death in 1866 in Washington, D.C., at which time a memorial address was made at a combined meeting of the House and Senate. It was not until 1891 that the suggestion was made that Lincoln's Birthday should be made a national holiday. The following year the State of Illinois made February 12 a legal holiday. Several other states followed suit, and year after year other states were added. Now Lincoln's Birthday is a legal holiday in thirty-eight states and in the Virgin Islands.

On the one hundredth anniversary of Lincoln's birth— 1909—there were celebrations all over America in his honor. That year, another famous American made the principal address at a Lincoln celebration in New York City. He was

Booker T. Washington, a Negro who had been given freedom because of Abraham Lincoln and the Emancipation Proclamation.

The one hundred and fiftieth anniversary of the birth of Lincoln was observed in 1959. Carl Sandburg, noted poet and biographer of Lincoln, made a speech on Lincoln to the House of Representatives in Washington, and a speech by Mayor Willi Brandt of West Berlin highlighted the observances at Springfield, Illinois. During the year the Sesquicentennial was also marked by the issuance of a set of three Lincoln stamps and by the dedication of a statue of the Emancipator. This monument, the largest statue of Lincoln ever erected, was placed on the highest point of the Lincoln Highway, twelve miles east of Laramie, Wyoming.

Annually in the tiny town of Hingham, near Norwich, England, a service is held to honor Abraham Lincoln on his birthday. Hingham is justly proud of the bust of Lincoln which was given by Americans to the little Hingham Church. Its inscription reads: *"In this parish for many generations lived the Lincolns, ancestors of the American ABRAHAM LINCOLN. To Him, greatest of that lineage."* Lincoln's ancestry has been traced back to one Robert Lincoln who died in Hingham in 1543. It was this man's great-grandson Samuel who emigrated to the American Colonies in 1637 and became a weaver at Hingham, Massachusetts, and it was Samuel's grandson, John, who was killed by Indians, leaving a five-year-old son, Thomas. Thomas Lincoln was Abraham's father.

Although it was his fate to be at the helm when this nation was launched upon the most tragic era of its career, Abraham Lincoln was far from being a warrior. He was a peace-loving man in every sense of the word, but his belief in peace was founded on his faith in the right. He believed slavery was not right. "As I would not be a slave, so I would not be a master," he said. He believed that the Union could be saved only by settling the question of slavery. No one dreaded more than he the issue toward which the slave problem was drawing the nation. But Lincoln knew, with his keen sense of foresight, that the Union would be dissolved if its differences were not settled once and for all. It was truly a question of "United we stand, divided we fall!" just as it had been in the War of Independence. In an address at Cleveland, Ohio, in 1861 Lincoln made this clear when he said, "If we do not make common cause to save the good old ship of the Union on this voyage, nobody will have a chance to pilot her on another voyage."

The Civil War was unquestionably Lincoln's great tragedy. His heart ached for every man on the battlefields, whether he was fighting for the North or the South. Every casualty was, to him, another drop of blood spilled to blot the history of a valiant new country. Lincoln's speech at Gettysburg testified what he hoped for in the ultimate outcome of the struggle. Those words with which he ended his speech, immortalized by their greatness, signify his faith in what that outcome was to be: "That this nation, under God, shall have a new birth of freedom, and that government of the people, by the people, for the people, shall not perish from the earth."

Lincoln did at least live to see the end of the war and to see his faith in freedom rewarded. But his joy was short-lived. On April 15, 1865, after having been shot at Ford's Theatre by John Wilkes Booth, he died in his fifty-seventh year.

But the memory of Abraham Lincoln did not die. His ideals as well as his accomplishments, the things he said as well as what he did, have lived on in the hearts of the people of his country and of all the world. Lincoln was wrong about one statement he made. In his address at Gettysburg he told his listeners, "The world will little note, nor long remember, what we say here." That speech of Lincoln's is far more likely to be remembered hundreds of years from now than any battle of the Civil War. It, like Lincoln, had the substance of true immortality.

Important Dates in the Life of Lincoln

1809:   Born February 12 in the State of Kentucky.

1816:   Family moved to Indiana, where he helped build log cabin.

1830:   Moved to Illinois. Started law career there. Became Postmaster.

1842:   Married Mary Todd of Lexington, Kentucky.

1847:   Elected to Illinois State Congress.

1857: Famous debate with Stephen A. Douglas
brought the slavery question to the fore.

1860: Nominated in Chicago for President by the
Republican Party and elected that November.

1863: Gettysburg Speech, November 19.

1864: Slavery abolished.

1865: On April 14, in Ford's Theatre, shot by
John Wilkes Booth. Died April 15.

Roses are red, violets are blue,
Sugar is sweet, and so are you!

St. Valentine's Day

FEBRUARY 14

That is a very, very old valentine rhyme which, as children, we printed dozens of times. On the day before the fourteenth of February we made valentines galore for Valentine's Day. We achieved surprising results with old wallpaper, a paste pot, and pictures cut from magazines and postcards. Somewhere on the valentine we always printed a verse, and on the back, the words *Guess who*. A big cardboard box with a huge slit in the top held these numerous, gay missives until St. Valentine's Day when, at the dinner table, the box was opened and the valentines were distributed. Added to these were real "store valentines" from older members of the family, decorated with red hearts, paper lace, cupids, and loving verses suitable to the day.

Valentine boxes are still popular with American children, for valentines can be bought inexpensively, so they buy them by the dozens. Children in the grade schools have their valentine boxes, from which the valentines are distributed at the close of school, while they send others by mail. Among grownups, boxes of candy decorated with big red hearts are more popular, and parties and dances are the custom on St. Valentine's Day. But, for the most part, February 14 has lost much of the romantic character it had in the olden days.

In times gone by, valentines sometimes cost as much as ten dollars apiece, and gorgeously extravagant creations they were, to be sure! A London magazine describes one of these, "in which a white-enameled Cupid appeared with wings picked out in silver amid a network of balusters, tassels, escallop-shells, seaweed, and monster tulips." About the time of the Civil War in America, the valentine was at the height of its popularity with young and old alike. A Boston periodical of 1863 says, "Indeed, with the exception of Christmas there is no festival throughout the year which is invested with half the interest belonging to this cherished anniversary."

Who started all this valentine sending that has been going on through hundreds of years, and who was St. Valentine, anyway?

Many hundreds of years ago in the days of the Roman

festivals to pagan gods, there was a feast called the *Lupercalia*. It was the custom at this feast for the young Romans to put into a box the names of young maidens and then draw the names out by chance. The girl whose name he drew became the young man's partner for the *Lupercalia*

festival. With the introduction of Christianity, the celebrations in honor of heathen gods were eradicated in every way possible, but the people had become so accustomed to the rituals of their various holidays and festivals that it was impossible to do away with them entirely. Previously a festival honoring Juno, goddess of women and marriage, and Faunus, or Pan, god of nature, the *Lupercalia* had always been celebrated on February 15. In the year A.D. 496, Pope Galasius of Rome chose a substitute patron for Christians. The new celebration was to honor a bishop by the name of Valentine who on February 14, about A.D. 270, had been executed on Palatine Hill, where once had stood an altar to Pan. Christians now honored St. Valentine on the day of his martyrdom, but St. Valentine's Day also took on many of the customs of the ancient *Lupercalia*.

There is very little known of the life of the patron saint of February 14, Bishop Valentine. Some historians have claimed that he has been confused with another St. Valentine, who lived during Emperor Claudius's time and was imprisoned for marrying couples secretly when the emperor, on some pretext, had forbidden the marriages to take place. The best authorities, however, identify our St. Valentine as the churchman who was beaten and beheaded on February 14 because he had cured his jail-keeper's daughter of blindness. He is buried in the church of St. Praxedes at Rome, where a gate was named for him, *Porto Valentini* (later named the *Porta del Popolo*).

Brand's *Popular Antiquities* claims that St. Valentine's

Day has been observed in England since 1446. In literature the holiday is mentioned by Chaucer and Shakespeare. It was Ophelia in Shakespeare's Hamlet who sang:

> *Good morrow! 'tis St. Valentine's Day*
> *All in the morning betime,*
> *And I a maid at your window,*
> *To be your Valentine!*

The oldest custom of the day in England and Scotland, because it had come down from the *Lupercalia,* was that of drawing names from an urn. But this practice has long since died out. In Norwich, England, St. Valentine's Day used to be a day for giving gifts. These were presented in the manner of May baskets and were left at the doorstep of the recipient. So general was the custom at one time that it was said the noise of the knockers of people leaving their baskets made a horrible din. In the town of Norfolk it was the custom for children to catch each other for valentines. They would say, "Good morrow, Valentine!" and if the speaker could repeat his words before he was given a reply, he was rewarded with a small gift. In Oxfordshire the boys and girls collected pennies by singing along the streets these words:

> *Good morning to you, Valentine,*
> *Curl your locks as I do mine,*
> *Two before and three behind,*
> *Good morrow to you, Valentine.*

In Derbyshire the girls used to look through the keyhole early on the morning of St. Valentine's Day and "if they saw only a single object or person they would remain unmarried all that year. If they saw, however, two or more objects or persons, they would be sure to have a sweetheart, and that in no distant time; but if fortune so favored them that by chance they saw a cock and a hen, they might be certain of being married before the year was out." In this place also there was the belief that if a maid would run around the church twelve times at midnight repeating:

> *I sow hempseed, hempseed I sow,*
> *He that loves me best come after me now,*

she would be sure to see her future husband!

There was an old saying that if snowdrops were brought into the house before St. Valentine's Day the single women of that house would remain unmarried all year! Other superstitions along this line are evident in the following extract from a young lady's diary for 1754:

Last Friday was Valentine's Day and the night before I got five bay-leaves, and pinned four of them to the four corners of my pillow, and the fifth to the middle; and then if I dreamt of my sweetheart, we should be married before the year is out. But to make it sure, I boiled an egg hard and took out the yolk, and filled it with salt; and when I went to bed ate it, shell and all, without speaking or drinking after it. We also wrote our lovers' names

47

upon bits of paper, and rolled them up in clay, and put them into water; and the first that rose up was to be our valentine.

To the young people of today a state of uncertainty about the future would be preferable to such drastic measures as those described!

There has always been a superstition among rural people that the birds selected their mates on St. Valentine's Day.

It is still the custom in England for children to go about on Valentine's Eve singing for pennies, apples, or oranges. They have different songs in various localities. One goes like this:

> *Good morrow, Valentine,*
> *A piece of bacon, and a piece of cheese*
> *And a bottle of wine.*
> *If you've got a penny in your pocket*
> *Slip it into mine.*
> *We used to come at eight o'clock*
> *And now we come at nine.*

In some sections of England, it is customary to eat a certain kind of bun made with caraway seeds and currants or plums. In Rutland these buns have been given to the boys and girls of the town on St. Valentine's Day for hundreds of years.

Young people in Denmark exchange valentines in a unique form. These are pressed snowdrops, and with the dried flower they send a greeting which they have composed themselves, in rhyme. Instead of signing their names they use a code of dots.

The Sicilians hold a happy festival on February 14. It is said that a young girl in Sicily should stand at her window for a half hour before the sun rises on the morning of St. Valentine's Day, and if she sees no one pass she will have to remain unmarried that year. But if a man should happen to come within sight of her watching eyes, it means that either he or someone closely resembling him will become her husband, and that within the year!

*America has furnished to the world
the character of Washington. And if our
American institutions had done nothing
else, that alone would have entitled them
to the respect of mankind.*

—DANIEL WEBSTER

Washington's Birthday

FEBRUARY 22

To know the history of our country is to know Washington. He stands justly with the greatest statesmen the world has ever known. Washington was born February 11, 1732, according to the old style calendar then still in use. The new style calendar adoption changed the date to February 22.

It is unusual for a famous person to have his birthday celebrated before his death, but that happened to George Washington. The first celebration of Washington's Birthday took place in Newport, Rhode Island, on February 11, 1781, eighteen years before his death. The day was made a holiday, with French troops parading the streets and cannons booming their salutes in honor of the Commanding General, beloved hero of a new nation. For several years February 11 was observed as Washington's Birthday, and then in 1790 New York and Richmond began to celebrate the new date, February 22. It is interesting to note that for a number of years the day was observed in some cities on the eleventh, in others on the twenty-second.

Washington's adopted daughter, Nellie Custis, was married on what proved to be his last birthday, February 22, 1799. The combined wedding and birthday must have been a memorable day at Mount Vernon. It is not hard to imagine the beautiful home of George and Martha Washington as it must have looked on that occasion, with many guests thronging the well-furnished rooms, hundreds of candles throwing a soft light over the scene, and huge fires blazing in the fireplaces to keep out the chill winter winds that blew up from the Potomac. Noted for its true Southern hospitality, Mount Vernon was a regal home. Today it is one of the show places of America.

Washington died that same year, on December 14. Although a vault was erected under the dome of the Capitol for his last resting place, his body was interred in the Mount Vernon family tomb. Washington's Tomb is said to be the most visited shrine in the United States, a half million persons annually paying tribute to the grave of our country's first President.

There are innumerable memorials to Washington in the United States, of which the most famous, of course, is the nation's capital, Washington, D.C. The State of Washington and at least twenty-three cities or towns have been named for him, and seven colleges bear his name. The Washington Monument, a beautiful white marble shaft more than 555 feet high, was begun in 1848 and completed in 1884. Forty years after it was started it was opened to the public, and since then millions of people have ascended this unusual structure and looked down upon the city of gleaming white buildings below.

Besides Mount Vernon, Washington's birthplace at Wakefield, Virginia (carefully restored), and his boyhood home have also been made into shrines. The latter is on the Rappahannock River near Fredericksburg, Virginia. George Washington spent his boyhood years there from the age of seven until he was fifteen. Still another memorial is the De Windt House at Tappan, New York, near the George Washington Bridge, this house having been General Washington's headquarters on several occasions during the Revolutionary War.

Throughout the nation, the public schools observe Washington's Birthday with appropriate programs. Perhaps the most unique celebration is that in Biddeford and Saco, Maine—where "tar-tub" fires have been burned on this day for two hundred years. This strange custom originated at the close of the Revolution through Squire Samuel Pierson, one of Washington's private clerks in the war. His birthday was the same as Washington's, and he probably wanted to celebrate the occasion in some unusual way. Tubs

filled with tar were set on fire and pulled through the town amid much shouting and cheering. Though the name of the "tar-tub" fires persists, they have gradually evolved into many individual barrel bonfires.

The greatest celebration of Washington's Birthday took place in 1932, the bicentennial year. The observance opened formally at midnight on New Year's Eve with the striking of a grandfather clock that had belonged to Washington's mother, Mary Ball Washington, which was heard by radio from coast to coast. Thus began a memorable year's celebration, for the two hundredth anniversary of the birth of

Washington was observed throughout the United States and its possessions, as well as in 259 cities in eighty-one countries of the world. The formal celebration lasted from February 21 until Thanksgiving Day, with special emphasis on holidays like Memorial Day, Flag Day, Independence Day, and Thanksgiving. New York City, for instance, started the bicentennial there on February 21 with parades, meetings, and special addresses, radio programs and plays, exhibits and flag displays. In Washington, D.C., the anniversary was opened on the same day with President Hoover's speech to Congress on George Washington, followed by the singing of "America" by twelve thousand voices.

Never had there been such a well-planned celebration of a national hero in any land! As Director of the United States George Washington Bicentennial Commission, Mr. Sol Bloom made it possible for every city and community, every school and organization in the country, to take part. The Commission had been created by Congress in 1924, and no stone was left unturned, no detail neglected, in making the anniversary year a success. The event also was observed in Italy, France, Germany, Japan, Poland, Australia, England, Cuba, and India. The Polish government presented President Hoover with an elaborately engraved stamp depicting George Washington in the center, with the Polish heroes of the American Revolution, Pulaski and Kosciusko, on either side.

A series of twelve special stamps issued by the United States Post Office commemorated the bicentennial year.

Each of the twelve stamps showed Washington as he has been painted or sculptured by a famous artist.

Among other outstanding achievements of the bicentennial year were the fourteen large murals painted by American artists to hang in the National Gallery, the collection and publication of Washington's entire writings, the planting of ten million trees in his honor, and a spectacular pageant at the foot of the Washington Monument lasting for three days, in which 10,000 persons participated.

Probably the most far-reaching result of the bicentennial was its educational effect. An intensive study of the life of Washington was made by millions of school children. They read biographies of him and studied his principles and the effect of those principles on the making of the nation. Surely his high ideals of government, his courage as a soldier, his patience as a commander, and his devotion to his country could not help but inspire hero worship in the hearts of many. For Abraham Lincoln, who took the presidency seventy-two years later, George Washington was a model upon whom much of his own life was molded. Although the lives of Washington and Lincoln were materially different, their ideals and aspirations were in many ways similar. Washington, being a man of great wealth, was accustomed to slavery, but he did not accept it in his own mind as being right. In a speech many years after Washington's death, President McKinley discussed the first President's views on slavery: "Washington's views on slavery were characterized by a high sense of justice and an exalted conscience. He was

55

the owner of slaves by inheritance, all his interests were affected by slavery, yet he was opposed to it, and in his will he provided for the liberation of his slaves. He set the example for emancipation. He hoped for, prayed for, and was willing to vote for what Lincoln afterward accomplished."

When George Washington was elected President of the United States in New York City in 1789, travel was so difficult that it took him seventeen days to make the journey from Virgina to New York for his inauguration. But what a unique and enviable position his was! The office he was to fill was highest in the land. He was to head a new nation that had been settled and colonized by brave, hardy groups of men and women and established by their valorous descendants. Washington, as he took the oath of office, must have realized the solemnity of the moment. After the inauguration he made a prayer for the new country for which he had fought and over which he was to preside. He had been a great soldier, and he was to be a great President.

Saint Patrick's Day

MARCH 17

Saint Patrick belongs to Ireland. Sure, 'n' all the saints in Heaven must know that that's a fact! Ireland—Saint Patrick—the shamrock! Their relationship is so close that it is, in itself, reminiscent of that three-leaved symbol, the shamrock. But, though Patrick is Ireland's patron saint, beloved by every true son of Erin, he was not a native Irishman, for he was not born on Irish soil. Considering that his is one of the best-loved names in history, the details of Saint Patrick's life are surprisingly vague, and most of the stories that have survived concerning him are flavored with legend. His biographers usually disagree on all the main facts—the date and place of his birth and death, for instance—but we

57

are able, in spite of their disagreements, to piece together a fairly coherent account of his exciting life.

He is thought to have been born about A.D. 387 in a small Roman town in what is now probably Wales. There is a wide difference of opinion concerning the country of his birth, that honor having been claimed by England, Scotland, and France as well as by Wales. He was born of a patrician family by the name of Sucat, and his father was a member of the magistracy of the town. The boy was named Maewyn; it was not until many years later that he was given the name of Patricius. From the time of his boyhood, he seemed predestined for adventure and achievement. The adventure began when, at the age of sixteen, he was captured by pirates and sold into slavery. He soon found himself in a strange land, in the county of Antrim in Ireland. It was a life spent entirely out in the open for, as a slave, he was put to work as a swineherd. It is thought that the six years spent in the wild new country furnished him with the inspiration that influenced the whole course of his life. It is pretty certain that it was at this time he determined to spend his life in an effort to free the people of that country from paganism. From his own *Confessions,* which have been translated from the Latin, Patrick tells how after six years of service he saw a vision and heard a voice saying, "Behold, a ship is ready for thee," and how he finally managed to escape from serfdom, secure passage on a boat as in his vision, and finally reach his own home.

Maewyn was then a young man of twenty-two years. With his mind firmly fixed on his purpose he set out to receive the training he needed. He spent four years at Tours, France, in study. But the serious young man was again halted in his life work when he was captured a second time and sent into slavery. From his *Confessions* we learn that it was during this time that he heard the voices of many people coming from the dark, mysterious forests of Ireland, bidding him to help them.

Patrick was enslaved only two months this time. After his return to his studies, by degrees he became priest, bishop, and statesman. Then in the year A.D. 431, after having received the ecclesiastical name of Patricius from Pope Celestine, he was at last sent by the Pope to Ireland, according to his wishes, to free the people from paganism and convert them to Christianity. It is believed that Saint Patrick landed at Wicklow Head in the spring of A.D. 432. One historian tells of this landing:

When Saint Patrick landed near Wicklow, the inhabitants were ready to stone him for attempting an innovation in the religion of their ancestors. He requested to be heard, and explained unto them that God is an omnipotent sacred Spirit, who created Heaven and Earth, and that the Trinity is contained in the Unity; but they were reluctant to give credit to his words. Saint Patrick, therefore, plucked a trefoil [shamrock] from the ground, and expostulated with the Hibernians: "Is it not as possible for the Father, Son, and Holy Ghost, as for these three leaves to grow upon a single stalk?" The the Irish were immediately convinced of their error, and were solemnly baptized by Saint Patrick.

It is doubtful, however, that Saint Patrick was so easily able to convince his listeners. It is said that he was forced back to his ship, after his first landing at Wicklow, and had to land farther along, at Lecale. But that Patrick's persistence was successful is too well known for dispute. His success was so overwhelming that he was able to establish 365 churches and as many schools and one or two colleges, consecrate at least two bishops, baptize approximately 120,000 persons, and Christianize the entire population of a country whose history up to that time had been one of complete paganism. Patrick was a man whose fearlessness was more

than a match for the Druids in spite of their previous un-
disputed hold on the people. The pagan priests were of
course his worst enemies, especially the *Druadh*. They were
the magicians or physicians among the people, steeped in
the art of their mysterious and terrible cult, ages old. The
Irish had for so long believed in the existence of spirits,
phantoms, and gods, who were all powers of evil, that it
was the only thing they could understand. Saint Patrick
must have been aware of this when he chose a trefoil to
illustrate to them in an understandable manner the Trinity
of the Christian God. For the trefoil was to the Druids not
just an ordinary clover. It had been assigned a magic power
by the *Druadh* and was thought of by the people as being
a symbol of magic.

All of the stories that have come down to us through the
ages concerning Saint Patrick have an air of mystery and
color about them. It is said that wherever he went Patrick
was preceded by a drummer, and that the mysterious beat of
the drum though the forests would announce to all who
heard it that the great foreign Bishop was approaching. The
strange and unusual was expected of him, and Patrick had
an amazing way of reaching the uncivilized people through
their imaginations.

The life of Saint Patrick after an almost unbelievable
career came to an end on March 17 in the district of Saul,
in the year 461, it is believed. When the news of his death
reached the people, they came flocking to his funeral by the
thousands. There were so many torches and candles carried

61

in the procession that it was said to be light as day at that place; and from that, probably, has sprung the story that during the days between his death and burial the sun never went down at all. According to most historians, Patrick was buried at Downpatrick in Ireland.

The best-known story of Saint Patrick is that which tells how he rid the land of Ireland of snakes. In Chambers's *Book of Days* we read: "The greatest of St. Patrick's miracles was that of driving the venomous reptiles out of Ireland, and rendering the Irish soil, forever after, so obnoxious to the serpent race that they instantaneously die on touching it."

These lines are quoted by Chambers from a poet in regard to another miraculous story of the saint:

> *Saint Patrick, as in legends told,*
> *The morning being very cold,*
> *In order to assuage the weather,*
> *Collected bits of ice together;*
> *Then gently breathed upon the pyre,*
> *When every fragment blazed on fire.*

He is attributed with having raised several people from the dead, one of them having been his own father.

It is said that Saint Patrick's Day is always clear because the saint had petitioned it so! Even today there is the belief that every alternate day after March 17 will be bright and sunshiny, and in Ireland and wherever the Irish live there is the popular belief that after Saint Patrick's Day it is time to plant the garden.

Since Patrick is Ireland's patron saint, March 17, commemorating the day of his death, is the most important day of the calendar in that country. For hundreds of years it has been celebrated with great joy and the gayest of ceremonies. Parades and speeches are the order of the day, after High Mass. The evenings are spent with music and dancing and general hilarity. The people try in every way to do as the old ballad bids them: "Saint Patrick's Day, we'll all be very gay."

It used to be the custom for the wealthy people of Ireland to brew ale in February and keep it until Saint Patrick's Day, when pickled salmon and oaten bread were eaten with it. The innkeepers would give a "Patrick's Pot"—a quantity of ale or whisky—to everybody, free! To "drown the shamrock" with a Patrick's Pot was an unvarying custom of every Saint Patrick's evening. Over the Patrick's Pot the jovial company wished each other health and riches, including "long leases and low rents."

"Drowning the shamrock" was done by the devotee of Saint Patrick dipping a shamrock in his glass of liquor, then touching it to the shamrock in his hatband. The shamrock, or trefoil (sometimes called hop-clover), grows in great abundance in Ireland and is often used there as a watercress. It is still believed by many to have curative powers, this belief having come down from the ancient Druids and been strengthened, probably, by the importance it assumed through Saint Patrick's connection with it. As the national emblem of Ireland, the shamrock forms a part of the British coat-of-arms. In the great British emblem, the rose is for England, the thistle for Scotland, and the shamrock for Ireland.

Symbols seem to have great significance among the Irish. One writer describes the *croiseog* worn in that country on Saint Patrick's Day. He says, "On this day every child throughout Ireland, excepting Connemara and some of the northern districts, is expected to wear upon the left breast a small disk intersected by crosses upon the surface and known as *croiseog* or 'favor.' In Connemara the *croiseog* is worn only by the women. They are of various designs and colors, but the general pattern is everywhere the same. . . . In Clare and Connemara there is usually but one cross, drawn upon the surface of the disk with the blood of the wearer, the blood being obtained by pricking the finger. The green is usually procured from grass and the yellow from the yolk of an egg."

Today in Ireland, as in years gone by, there can be seen on Saint Patrick's Day picturesque old women selling the three-leaved trefoil. "Buy my shamrock, green shamrock!" they call to passers-by. On this day it is customary for the rich to give to the poor. In Dublin the very elite of the upper classes are invited to an impressive ball at Dublin Castle. It is held in a large ballroom known as Saint Patrick's Hall, which has been the scene of this annual social function for many years. The ball is attended each year now by the President of the Republic of Ireland.

There is always a big parade in Dublin, as well as a true Irish dance festival. One great difference between the old-time Saint Patrick's Day celebrations and those of today is

that now on March 17 there is little or no "drowning of the shamrock," and instead of the old green flag of tradition with the proverbial harp, there is a new flag that floats over the country—green, white, and orange, the flag of the free country of Eire! To the freedom-loving people of the country of Saint Patrick, it is the most beautiful in all the world. If it had not been for Saint Patrick and his perseverance, it might not wave today.

Saint Patrick's Day has been observed in New York City

since 1762. The celebrations staged by the Irish in the cities of New York, Chicago, San Francisco, and Boston exceed those of good old Dublin. Saint Patrick's Cathedral is always the focal point of interest in the spectacular parades in New York. The Friendly Sons of Saint Patrick, the organization that sponsors the New York Saint Patrick's Day parade, begin work on it right after New Year's. It is a thrilling sight. Some twenty thousand marchers make their way down Fifth Avenue in the early spring sunshine to the tunes of numerous bands. "When Irish Eyes are Smiling," "Wearing of the Green," and other favorites bring hearty cheers from the throng of half a million spectators. Young students of the parochial schools whose fife and drum corps add to the music of the procession lend color to the scene with their brilliant red capes. Thousands of parading children are dressed appropriately in green, and the kilts of the pipers are green in honor of the Emerald Isle, while shamrocks and green hats and flags or some other bit of the color is worn by those who watch the parade.

In Rome, the observance of Saint Patrick's Day takes a different form. In the churches there, the day is celebrated with much pomp and ceremony to commemorate his sainthood. And perhaps this is what the good saint would have liked best of all—remembering the Church, for which he lived, and preserving his day as a Saint Day.

Easter

MARCH OR APRIL

Easter is the time of year for chocolate bunnies and eggs. It seems natural enough for us to eat these at the accustomed time, but do we ever stop to think why? Why should we have bunnies, of all things, at Easter? There *is* a reason.

The bunny is really a hare, and according to legends of far-off Egypt, the hare is a symbol of the moon. Everyone knows that the date of Easter is determined by the moon. In the year A.D. 325 Constantine had the uncertain date of this holy day settled for all time by taking the matter before the Council of Nicea. The worthy and wise ones of the Council decided that Easter should fall upon *the first*

Sunday after the first full moon after the twenty-first day of March. And so the hare, or bunny, has come into prominence because of the moon's importance in reckoning Easter.

As for Easter eggs, they are so closely bound up with Easter that it would be like taking the Christmas tree away from a Christmas celebration to eliminate eggs from an Easter festival. Wherever this holiday is observed, eggs play some part in the celebration. The egg is the symbol of new life, and that probably is why it has come to hold so much significance at the commemoration of the Resurrection. For hundreds of years dyed eggs have been exchanged as a token of peace at Easter. In fact, we can trace the custom of egg-giving back to the ancient Egyptians, long before the time of Christ. The custom was prevalent among the ancient Hebrews also, for the paschal egg held an important place at the festive board of the Passover.

In the eighteenth century, egg-races were the main event at the Easter fetes in certain parts of France. The winner of the race was given a hogshead of cider as a prize.

Egg games and egg races have not lost their popularity even today. American children often join in egg-rolling contests on Easter Monday. The most famous of these is held on the White House south lawn in the nation's capital for hundreds of children who are guests of the President and his wife for the occasion.

In New York's Central Park, egg-rolling contests have been held since 1947, with hundreds of small boys and girls

competing for exciting prizes donated by the city's department stores.

In England, especially in the northern shires, egg rolling
is an annual event. The eggs are saved all through Holy
Week for the sport on Easter Day. Children of Scotland
paint hard-boiled eggs and roll them down a grassy slope

on Easter morning. This, they say, represents the rolling away of the stone from the tomb of the risen Christ. Children of Bohemia and Germany also like to roll eggs at Easter time. The Germans often roll the eggs on tracks made of sticks. The sport starts at midnight and lasts until near dawn on Easter morning.

In Ireland at dawn on Easter Day eggs are eaten to break the Fast of Lent, while eggs in Scotland are used by the boys and girls for a game of ball! In the Tyrol, children carry baskets and torches and sing Easter carols as they travel through the valley from farmhouse to farmhouse on Easter Eve. At each place they are given bright colored eggs to put into their baskets, the farmers' wives having vied with each other in coloring and decorating them, even printing mottoes on their hard shells. The children of Iraq gather all the eggs they can during the forty days of Lent, selling them at Eastertide in the market places.

The boys and girls of many of our rural sections here in America save eggs during Lent, too, coloring them for Easter baskets, and children in Belgium make nests of hay and hide them in the grass on the day before Easter, knowing full well that Easter morning will show them overflowing with eggs—both dyed ones and those made of chocolate.

In Italy, eggs take on a more reverential role. They are carried to church by the hundreds and blessed by the priests. Then they are taken home and given the center of the table as the main dish at the Easter Feast. Everything on the table is arranged around the eggs—the food, the best silver and flowers. Sometimes they number as many as two hundred, all colored in the most brilliant and arresting hues of red, blue, purple, and gold. Visitors to the house during Easter Week must not refuse this sacred food of the Resurrection.

The people of the Ukraine, according to custom, like to rub the dyed red eggs against their cheeks to make them glow, adding to their look of happiness at the Easter Feast. In Russia, before the Soviet government changed the custom, rich and poor alike exchanged dyed eggs at Easter time with the greeting, "Christ is risen!" Here, too, the eggs had been blessed at the church where, early on Easter morning, it was customary for the priests to bless the food which the people had piled in great colorful heaps—hard bright eggs and pyramids of curds lavishly embellished.

> *One-a-penny buns,*
> *Two-a-penny buns,*
> *One-a-penny, two-a-penny,*
> *Hot cross buns!*

So sings the bun peddler in England. Nowhere in the world are hot cross buns sold or eaten except during Lent. They are, most especially, an item of Friday fare. With the sign of the cross made in their delicious top crusts, they have become emblematic of that Friday many hundreds of years ago when Christ died on the Cross. In olden times the eating of hot cross buns was said to protect the house from fire for the ensuing year. Some even believed that, ground up, the crumbs of the buns could be added to water and used for medicinal purposes the year round. From *Poor Robin's Almanack* we are told:

> *Good Friday comes this month, the old woman runs*
> *With one- or two-a-penny hot cross buns,*
> *Whose virtue is, if you believe what's said,*
> *They'll not grow mouldy like the common bread.*

Today in France it is customary to eat pancakes on Shrove Tuesday and Ash Wednesday. This practice is also observed in many places in America. In old Russia, cakes fried in butter and called *blinnies* were eaten by everyone during the week preceding Lent, and in Switzerland the special food for this time was *Fastnacht* cake, made with caraway seeds. Strangely enough, the custom of eating buns, pancakes, and the like at the Easter season emanated from the pagan practice, many centuries before, of eating cakes in honor of the goddess Eostre at the time of the vernal equinox.

Eostre was the Anglo-Saxon name for the Teutonic goddess of spring, Ostera. There is no doubt that the fair goddess had considerable influence on the early Christians' naming of Easter. The pagan observance of the awakening of Earth from her long winter's sleep was naturally adaptable to the symbolism of the Awakening or Resurrection of the Christians' Lord from three days' sleep in the tomb. Thus the holiest of all Christian holidays derived its name from a pagan festival.

72

Many of the Easter customs among people of foreign lands would seem strange indeed to us who are not accustomed to them, but to those who observe them they are an inherited element in their lives. Dancing in Spain on Easter Day, for instance, so different from our own observance of the holy day, is truly a national characteristic of the music-loving Spaniards. Ukrainian girls in their country dance the traditional *hahilki,* accompanied by the happy voices of the dancers raised in the merry *hahilki* songs. In Ireland, too, there is dancing on Easter Sunday. Over the entire countryside old and young alike compete for a prize cake with their dancing, and long hours of fun and excitement prevail before the winning couple "takes the cake."

Among the Tyrolese farmers there is apt to be dismay when Shrove Tuesday comes around. With the same spirit of mischief that invades our own rural districts on Halloween, on Shrove Tuesday the prank-loving boys of that place lead the farmer's cow into his kitchen garden, hide his gate, and hoist his cart and wheelbarrow to the roof of his house!

During Lent in Hungary, social life for adults is at a standstill, but for the young people there is a unique game played with fire called *sajbozas*. A combination of ritual and sport, it is played in an open field or pasture in the evening on the first Sunday of Lent. The girls set fire to a small hut of timber that has been built beforehand. From this, after the blaze has somewhat subsided, the boys heat *sajbo* rings in the hot flames. With a clever twist of a stick they send the red-hot rings flying through the darkness, with an effect not unlike the fireworks of our Fourth of July.

In Suffolk, England, there used to be a quaint custom of choosing twelve old women of the village to play ball on Easter Monday, the ball game coming to an end at sunset. The significance of this custom died out long before its observance did. Another old English custom was "lifting." This strange byplay took place on the two days following Easter. On Easter Monday the men carried a silk-lined chair, adorned with flowers and streamers, merrily through the streets of the village in search of fair damsels! When they met one, she was made to sit in the chair, which was then lifted high in the air amid shouts of laughter and shrieks from the fair victim. There was only one means of escaping her captors, and that was to pay a forfeit, often a kiss. On the next day the positions were reversed; the chairs were carried by the women and the men were the victims!

"Clipping the church" was once popular in England at Easter. Hosts of children all dressed in their best for the occasion stood around the church with their backs to the building. Joining hands, they formed a complete circle, with the church or small chapel in the center of the ring. Each church in the village was "clipped," or embraced, with serious ceremony.

Until the time of James II, it was customary on Maundy Thursday for the sovereign of England to wash the feet of at least twelve paupers, representing the act of Jesus washing the feet of the twelve disciples at the Last Supper on the day before Good Friday. In history we read of this ritual being performed by good Queen Bess at the age of thirty-nine, when she washed the feet of thirty-nine paupers. Maundy Thursday plays an important part in the ceremonies of Holy Week in the Catholic Church. Among the Volhynian Ukrainians on that day many people bathed in the river, for it was believed during that time to have curative powers.

Ukrainians always observed the Easter season for two weeks, beginning with Willow Sunday (Palm Sunday). The first week was observed with reverence, the second devoted to social activity. Usually the farmers went back to their labors on the Thursday after Easter, but all the evenings were spent in visiting, dancing, and card-playing. In fact, the festive evenings continued until Ascension Day.

There is a peculiar ceremony that takes place in Greece on Good Friday. A wooden effigy of Jesus, followed by a procession of people, is carried through the streets with great ceremony and then given burial. This funeral, of course, is to express sorrow over Jesus' death on the Cross.

In Mexico effigies of Judas Iscariot, the disciple who betrayed Jesus, are severely dealt with at high noon on Holy Saturday. Thousands of Judas Iscariots, of all sizes and shapes and of hideous caricature, are hanged, beaten, burned, and otherwise punished by the Mexicans who throng the streets for the occasion.

75

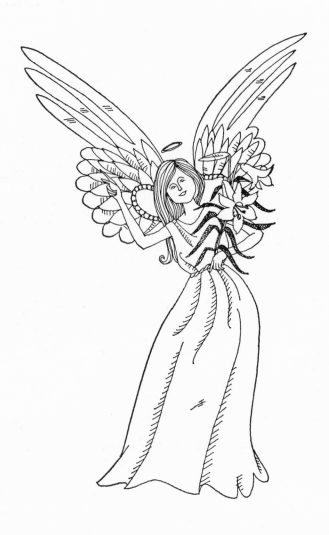

The French people, with their love for fetes and their enthusiasm over all holidays, celebrate Easter with religious dignity, observing Lent in the manner of the Roman Catholic Church. But the forty days of Lent are preceded by carnivals all over France, the most famous of which is held on Shrove Tuesday, known as Mardi gras. In Paris there is a grand carnival on Mid-Lent Sunday at which beauty queens are chosen to preside, and a fatted ox is the main feature of the colorful procession that winds its way through the famous streets of Paris. Many years ago, Easter was also the first of the new year, and one still occasionally hears the greeting "Happy New Year!"

It seems strange for us to think of Easter as being any different in this country from our present conception of it, but it has been only in the past seventy-five years that the churches of all denominations have observed Easter with any marked ceremony. At first it was only the Catholic churches that kept it. Maryland and Louisiana, because they were settled by Catholics, were the first states to observe Easter as a church festival. The New England states were the last to acknowledge it as a holiday.

Sunrise services at dawn on Easter Day have become an established feature of an American Easter. One of the first places in the United States to have observed this custom was Bethlehem, Pennsylvania. About three o'clock on Easter morning the Moravian Trombone Choir sends a message through the still, clear air to the people of the town from the steeple of the church, calling them to the service. Thousands of men, women, and children throng into the old Moravian Burying Ground beyond the church to await the dawn of Easter Day. "Christ is risen!" The voices sing the message to the accompaniment of the trombones as the sun appears over the surrounding purple hills. The dawn of another

Easter is greeted with new hope by these people, whose ancestors established the new Bethlehem and the Moravian Church in America.

In the State of Hawaii the same custom was wholeheartedly adopted years ago. In Honolulu every year there is a glorious Easter sunrise service held at the Punchbowl, a volcanic crater which stands, passive now, overlooking the city.

Sunrise services in Oklahoma at a place near Lawton feature the "Oklahoma Oberammergau" Easter play, attracting each year about ten thousand spectators.

It would take too long to tell of the beautiful and solemn religious services in the great churches and cathedrals over all the Christian world—of the magnificence of Easter at St. Peter's Cathedral in Rome, or of the pilgrimages to Jerusalem, the Holy City. In America, with well-trained choirs in towns and cities rendering Bach Masses and inspiring hymns of the Resurrection, and millions of people filling the churches to overflowing on Easter Sunday, this is without doubt the holiest of all our holidays. The religious observance of Easter is surely the most significant "custom" of all, for it commemorates that very first Easter more than nineteen hundred years ago when the angel of the Lord spoke from a sepulchre garden:

"He is not here: for he is risen."

April Fools' Day

April 1 can hardly be called a holiday, but it is one of those days of the calendar that refuse to be relegated to the place of just an ordinary day. After at least three hundred years of being the one day in the year's 365 when it is permissible to "befool" people, the custom still persists. Though All Fools' Day is in no way recognized by governments or encouraged by our public schools, and is seldom mentioned by writers, and certainly never praised in song or verse, it continues to hold its own in the minds of the people. On this day, from the time we get up in the morning until we go to bed, we can expect to fall prey to an April Fools' joke.

Back in 1760 these lines were written in *Poor Robin's Almanack*:

> *The first of April, some do say,*
> *Is set apart for All Fools' Day;*
> *But why the people call it so*
> *Nor I, nor they themselves, do know.*
> *But on this day are people sent*
> *On purpose for pure merriment.*

"Nor I, nor they themselves, do know" is as true today as it was then! The origin of this day is vague, the reasons for its observance having long been lost while its customs still prevail. There are evidences of All Fools' Day's being observed in England as early as the seventeenth century; it is thought to have been copied by the English from the French.

Although there are other conjectures concerning its origin, the one that follows seems to be the one most accepted by historians.

From time immemorial the vernal equinox has been observed by all kinds of people. It occurs around March 21. Until the time of the Gregorian Calendar, adopted in the sixteenth century, March 21 was also the beginning of the New Year. In those days the New Year ushered in a whole week of celebrations, and the last, or eighth, day of the festivities was devoted to the exchange of gifts. In the year 1582 Pope Gregory introduced a new calendar. March 21 was no longer the beginning of the New Year, and April

1 was no longer the most important day in the combined New Year and vernal equinox celebrations. But in those days news traveled very slowly, and consequently people continued to celebrate April 1 as the last glorious day of the New Year celebrations. Greetings were exchanged, and gifts given as before. But these people who still clung to the old calendar, either through ignorance or just through die-hard custom, soon became known as April fools. And thus it was that in France the first day of April came gradually to develop into a day of fooling and being fooled. The custom then spread into England and beyond.

The most popular form of fooling has always been to send the victim of the jest on some fruitless errand. Quoting again from *Poor Robin's Almanack*:

> . . . *In sending fools to get intelligence*
> *One seeks hen's teeth in farthest part of the town;*
> *Another pigeon's milk; a third a gown*
> *From strolling cobbler's stall, left there by chance;*
> *Thus lead the giddy tribe a merry dance.*
> *And to reward them for their harmless toil,*
> *The cobbler 'noints their limbs with stirrup oil.*
> *Thus by contrivers' inadvertent jest,*
> *One fool exposed makes pastime for the rest.*

In certain parts of England the time for playing April Fools' jokes is limited to the morning hours. If anyone should forget this rule and play a joke after the noon hour, the fooler becomes the fool! In Hampshire they say, "April

Fools's gone past; You're the biggest fool at last." Many are the witless errands the poor unsuspecting April noddie is sent upon. The person who so far forgets his dates as to "fall" for the jests of the first of April has earned many nicknames. In England, besides being a noddie, he is called a gawby, a gobby, or an April gob! In Scotland he is called an April-gowk, and there a gowk is a cuckoo! When the Scots send a victim on a foolish errand they say he is hunting the gowk.

The French are likely to send the April fool for some "sweet vinegar" or "a stick with only one end"! In France the person fooled on April 1 is called an April fish, *un poisson d'Avril*. This expression seems very appropriate since he "bites" on the joke and is "caught." But it is likely the *fish* has been borrowed from the sign of the zodiac, *Pisces*. In Provence on this day everybody eats peas. In years gone by April Fools' victims were sent to the Convent of Chartreux in Provence to ask for *pois chiches*. It seems that because of a vow made previously by the convent fathers, peas were given to all who asked for them.

In Lisbon, Portugal, All Fools' Day is observed on the Sunday and Monday preceding Lent. There the people threw ashes or flour into each other's faces, a most peculiar custom, the significance of which is unknown.

In India there is a day corresponding to All Fools' Day, called *Holi*. A celebration of the equinox, it is observed on March 31 and is so similar to April Fools' Day that it seems more than likely that they have had the same origin. Brand, in his *Popular Antiquities,* tells us, "During the Holi, when mirth and festivity reign among the Hindus of every class, one subject of diversion is to send people on errands and expeditions that are to end in disappointment, and raise a laugh at the expense of the person sent."

There is a funny story told by historians about an April Fools' joke that was played in London many years ago. Several days before the first of April, invitations were sent to many of the city's most prominent persons. They read:

Tower of London—
Admit Bearer and Friend
to view annual ceremony of Washing the White Lions
on Sunday, April 1, 1860.
Admittance only at White Gate.

Many cabs drove around Tower Hill that Sunday morning searching for the White Gate! It was said that those who lived in the vicinity were greatly disturbed by all the noise and very curious, too, as to what it was all about.

Another story comes down to us from history. It tells how Francis, Duke of Lorraine, and his wife were being held in captivity at Nantes, France. On the first day of April they disguised themselves as peasants and at an early hour of the morning attempted to pass through the city gates. All went well until the guard, informed of their identity, was told to give word to the sentry that those two were in reality Francis and his wife. But when the guard heard it, he shouted with laughter and cried, "April Fool!"

83

The word flew along the lines to the guards there, and all considered it a huge April Fools' joke. However, when the governor heard it he was suspicious. But too late. The Duke and his wife had escaped because of the fact that the day they had chosen for their escape was April 1, All Fools' Day.

Arbor Day

DATE VARIES IN DIFFERENT STATES

The founder of Arbor Day, J. Sterling Morton, expressed his feeling about the holiday in these words: "Other holidays repose upon the past; Arbor Day proposes for the future."

The planting of trees, to which this day is dedicated, is indeed an act of "proposing" for the future. From this motivation has come a great program of reforestation, soil and water conservation, and beauty to benefit our land. It would be hard to think of any holiday on our calendar that has done more for our nation. To understand this, we must try to visualize what America would be today without its vast forests and what they mean to our citizens. It has been

85

estimated that each one of us, in his lifetime, uses the wood that has been produced by three hundred mature trees.

The first Arbor Day in America was observed in Nebraska on April 10, 1872. In that year J. Sterling Morton, then a member of the State Board of Agriculture, introduced a resolution in the State Legislature which provided "That Wednesday, the 10th day of April, 1872, be . . . especially set apart and consecrated to tree planting in the State of Nebraska and the State Board of Agriculture hereby name it Arbor Day." The resolution was adopted at that meeting, and at the same time prizes were offered, one to an individual and another to the society that planted the greatest number of trees. As a result, more than a million trees were planted in the state on the first Arbor Day. Within the next sixteen years more than 350 million trees were planted, completely transforming a state that was previously a land of vast, treeless prairies. Because of this, Nebraska has come to be known as the Tree Planters' State. Later, Nebraska changed its Arbor Day to April 22, the birthday of the founder, J. Sterling Morton.

It was almost ten years before other states became interested in the Arbor Day movement, and then Ohio and North Dakota instituted Arbor Day. That year, 1882, Ohio was holding a National Forestry Convention in Cincinnati, where the idea was discussed and the advantages pointed out to other states. Two years later, at a National Education Association convention in Connecticut, a resolution was

introduced to the effect that "In view of the valuable results
of Arbor Day work in the six States where such a day has
been observed, alike upon the school and the home, this
Association recommends the general observance of Arbor
Day for schools in all our States." In 1887 Ontario, Canada,
began to observe an Arbor Day on the first Friday in May;
the following year New York State took it up, and grad-

ually all the states followed suit. Hawaii has had an Arbor Day since 1905.

Arbor Day is a legal holiday in only three states: in Florida, where it is observed on the third Friday in June, and in Nebraska and Utah, where it is celebrated in April. But in every state, as well as in the District of Columbia and Puerto Rico, it is proclaimed by the Governor or by the Board of Education. Although the dates vary in different parts of the country, it is usually observed in the spring. A few states celebrate two Arbor Days, and some combine it with Bird Day. In California it is on Luther Burbank's birthday, March 7.

Every year on March 26 Spain celebrates the Fete of the Tree, *Fiesta del Arbol.* This Arbor Day began in 1895, when the youthful King Alfonso planted a pine sapling at a ceremony near Madrid. Germany plants trees on Whitsunday. Palestine observes an Arbor Day annually on February 15.

The ancient Aztec Indians used to have a very nice custom of planting a tree whenever a child was born, a practice that Indians of other tribes continued.

An old Colonial custom demanded that a new bride bring a tree from her father's property to plant beside her new home. Sentimental attachment prompted the young woman to take great care of the new tree to see that it did not die after it was transplanted.

Planting trees is, of course, the purpose of Arbor Day, and many of these are planted as memorials. When the day was first observed in Cincinnati in 1882, school children of that city planted a grove of trees in Eden Park. It was known as Author's Grove because each tree was named for an author, a statesman, or some other famous person.

An enthusiastic promoter of Arbor Day was Dr. Birdsey G. Northrup of Connecticut. He not only traveled all over America but in Europe and Asia as well, lecturing and urging people to beautify the world by planting trees. He even offered prizes—a dollar to any child who planted five trees. Civic organizations in cities, towns, and suburbs, as well as the General Federation of Women's Clubs, have urged the same thing and have done a great deal of good in planting shade trees along the streets and highways. Trees also have been planted on the lawns of schools, churches, hospitals, and near many other public buildings.

The responsibility of planting a tree, however, doesn't end on Arbor Day. Trees must have good care all the year round. In many places Boy Scout troops are assigned the responsibility of caring for the trees that have been planted on Arbor Day, and in some cases a class in school will assume this duty for the year.

In 1924 a law was passed enabling landowners to receive forest-tree seeds and plants from the government—one of the biggest aids the nonforested sections of the United States have received.

The estimated combined area of America's 150 national forests amounts to more than 170 million acres. A government pamphlet on *Famous Trees* says:

In the United States there is abundant tree growth of the most useful species. The Nation has been quite literally nurtured in a wooden cradle, and its progress has been largely due to the contributions of the forest. The pioneers cut paths through the wilderness—from east to west and from north to south—and the forest harvest has gone into home and community building.

On all sides there is abundant evidence that forests are essential to civilized man's welfare. The individual tree, however, has an even more intimate part to play in human experience, a part so universal that every country has its famous tree citizens.

The old, old Aztec custom of planting a tree at the birth of a child is as symbolic as it is appropriate, for nothing in all nature seems more endowed with the spirit of life than the tree. As an embryo, it is gently nurtured in the warm pocket of Mother Earth until the seedling has reached maturity. In infancy it reaches its slender green tendrils toward the light of the sun, seeking strength and growth; like a child it shoots up to surprising tallness, growing week by week, month by month, and year by year, to adult stature. Then, in the dignity of maturity, it stands sometimes for centuries, a regal monument to the miracle of creation, lending beauty and honor to the world it graces.

A List of Famous Trees in America *

Washington Live Oak. Charleston, South Carolina. Washington visited Charleston in 1791, and here, so the story goes, was an honored guest in the beautiful plantation home of the distin-

---

* Compiled from *Famous Trees,* a publication of the U.S. Department of Agriculture.

guished Pinckney family. He heard the mistress of the household order her gardener to cut down the large oak that obstructed the view from the new portico. Washington, great tree lover that he was, expressed the wish that the tree be spared. It was.

Washington Elm Grandchild. A descendant of the Washington Elm at Cambridge, Massachusetts (now dead), was planted as a Washington Bicentennial tree on the grounds of the State Capitol in Hartford, Connecticut, on March 31, 1933. The Washington Elm at Cambridge was the tree under which the leader of the American Revolutionary forces assumed command in 1775.

Lincoln Memorial Hackberry. Decorah, Iowa. It was planted in memory of Abraham Lincoln by John Finn on April 27, 1865, the day that Governor Stone of Iowa set aside as a day of mourning for Lincoln. On that day Finn went into the woods, found a small hackberry tree, and transplanted it to a spot in front of his home. It grew to be one of the most magnificent trees in Iowa.

Lafayette Sycamore. Near Baltimore Pike, on a hill two hundred yards east of the Brandywine Baptist Church, near Chadds Ford, Delaware County, Pennsylvania. It is close to the house occupied by General Lafayette as his headquarters before the Battle of the Brandywine, September 10 and 11, 1777.

Maple. Planted in memory of Juliette Low, founder of the Girl Scouts of America, at Eighteenth Street and New York Avenue, NW, Washington, D.C., by the Girl Scouts of the District of Columbia.

J. Sterling Morton Elm. United States Capitol Grounds, planted in memory of the founder of Arbor Day, by Chief Forester R. Y. Stuart, in 1932. Another is an elm planted by the Nebraska Society at 1214 Sixteenth Street, NW, Washington, D.C., headquarters of the American Tree Association.

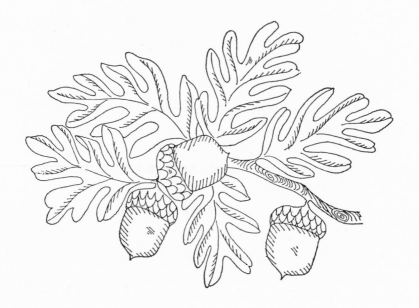

Friendship Elm (English elm). Planted by the Duke of Windsor, then Prince of Wales, in Central Park, New York City, in 1920. It is one hundred feet from the spot where his grandfather planted an American elm in 1860.

Penn Treaty Elm. At Shackamaxon, Pennsylvania, which is now in the Kensington section of Philadelphia, memorable as the place where William Penn concluded his famous treaty with the Indians in 1682. The elm was nearly three hundred years old when felled by a storm in 1810. It is perpetuated to the fourth generation, there being seven of its descendants growing in one place, the campus of Haverford College, Haverford, Pennsylvania.

Charter Oak. At Hartford, Connecticut, it stood in front of Governor Wyllys' mansion, built in 1638. The charter of the Connecticut Colony, granted by King Charles II in 1662, is supposed to have been hidden in the oak by a patriot when Sir Edmund Andros demanded its surrender in 1687, at the command of King James II. The charter served Connecticut as a constitution from 1662 to 1816 and conveyed to the colony all the land "from the said Narragansett Bay on the east to the South Sea on the west." The tree blew down in a light gale on August 21, 1856. The hole that concealed the charter had been enlarged enough to hold twenty-five men. Pieces of the wood were made into gavels, picture frames, and even chairs, one of which stands in the senate chamber of the State Capitol.

Council Oak. At Sioux City, Iowa, believed to have been 150 years old when Lewis and Clark saw it on their way to the Pacific coast and there held council with the Indians.

Hendrick Hudson's Tulip Tree. Inwood Park, northern end of Manhattan Island, at the mouth of the Harlem River, New York City. Hudson entered this inlet in 1609 and may have met the Indians there. The tree is the only living thing on the island that was there during Hudson's time.

Lombardy Poplar. Planted over two hundred years ago at Fort Niagara, Niagara Falls, New York, by the French occupants. It is the sole survivor of a group of these trees planted at the time. This is the only United States Army Post flying three flags—the French, British, and United States.

Louisa May Alcott Elms. In front of the Alcott home, the Orchard House, Concord, Massachusetts, and the little grove of pines and spruces just beyond it. The author of *Little Women* once lived under the shade of the elms. And among the whispering pines Hawthorne walked, thought, and wrote, or conversed with his friend, Thoreau.

Joyce Kilmer Memorial Forest. A four-thousand-acre tract of virgin forest near Lake Santeetlah in the Nantahala National Forest, southwestern North Carolina, was dedicated on July 30, 1936, to the poet who wrote "Trees."

Avery Oak. At Dedham, Massachusetts. It bears the distinction of having been selected as suitable material for the celebrated and much-honored frigate *Old Ironsides.* The amount offered was $70, but the offer was refused because the owner's wife greatly admired the tree.

Mothers of America Tree. European white birch, to memorialize mothers of the nation. Planted east of the United States Capitol Building by the American Forestry Association. It was chosen because of its beauty and dignity.

Road of Remembrance. A thousand elms planted along eight miles of road near Seattle, as the beginning of Memorial Way. Dedicated to the soldiers of the State of Washington who died during World War I.

Famous Weeping Birch. Flushing, Long Island. Said to be the origin of all trees of its kind in the eastern part of the United States.

Black Walnut Tree. Mount Vernon, Virginia. Its nuts have been taken for planting, by Boy Scouts, all over the country as memorial trees to George Washington.

General Sherman Bigtree. Sequoia National Park, California. It has a diameter of 36½ feet or a circumference of nearly 115 feet, a height of 272.4 feet, a volume of 600,120 board feet, and it is between three thousand and four thousand years old. Two other immense trees of this type are General Grant Bigtree, of General Grant National Park, and Grizzly Giant Bigtree, in Yosemite National Park, this last estimated at 3,800 years old.

Redwood. Humboldt State Redwood Park, near Dyerville, Humboldt County, California. It is said to be "the tallest tree now known." It is 364 feet high. This redwood has been dedicated to the founders of Save-the-Redwoods League and is therefore called the Founders Tree.

"Sovereign Cypress." In the dense swamp between Sanford and Longwood, Florida. It is supposed to have been a denizen of this section before Ponce de Leon sought the Fountain of Youth. There is space enough for a roadway to be cut through the trunk. Its estimated age is three thousand years.

Pan-American Day

APRIL 14

Here is a holiday that belongs to two great continents, the Americas! The United States, Mexico, and the republics of Central and South America are the nations that gave this young holiday its birth, proclaim it annually, and observe it hopefully—the objective a closer bond of mutual understanding and cooperation among the neighboring countries.

A great Teacher left this commandment to the world: "Love thy neighbor as thyself." Unfortunately, the commandment for many centuries meant little or nothing as applied to *nations as neighbors*. In ages past, with communication difficult and with differences in language and cus-

96

tom, it was almost impossible for nations to be neighborly. In those days there was some excuse for unfamiliarity with the rest of the world.

A writer in Buenos Aires in connection with Pan-American Day has said, "To understand each other we need only to know each other." That is true of all nations. In educating the young people of the world to this idea we are taking a definite step toward world peace. For this reason Pan-American Day is very important to all the peoples of the American republics, and especially to the young people who are learning to know their neighbors.

Pan-American Day is still a young holiday. At a meeting of the members of the Pan American Union on May 7, 1930, the governing board adopted a resolution declaring "that the Governments, members of the Pan American Union, designate April 14th as *Pan-American Day* and that the national flags be displayed on that date." And so it was that April 14, 1931, was the first Pan-American Day to be observed as a holiday. It was celebrated throughout America. President Hoover asked that the day be observed with appropriate ceremonies in all the schools, and that the flag be flown from all public buildings.

This was not, however, the beginning of Pan-Americanism. The first Pan-American conference of any importance was held in 1826 at Panama, when the governments of the Spanish colonies of South America and Central America were represented at a meeting. The United States sent no delegates to that, or to other conferences which followed, until 1889. In that year—when all countries of the American republics were represented—the union was organized. The conference lasted for six months! It was held in Washington, D.C., and James G. Blaine, who was then Secretary of State of the United States, was made Chairman of the union, which called itself The Commercial Bureau of American Republics.

In 1910 the name was changed to the Pan American Union. This organization took place on April 14, 1889, and it was for that reason that in 1930 the date April 14 was chosen as Pan-American Day. From the time of its organization the Pan American Union was a peace-loving and hopeful body, meeting for discussions of national and international problems concerning themselves and their affairs. In 1901 there was a Pan-American Exposition at Buffalo, New York, to demonstrate our new consciousness of our Southern neighbors. The Exposition "to celebrate the progress made in industries, science, and art by American republics during the nineteenth century" was an affair of spectacular beauty. Travelers from many lands came to see the "Rainbow City," so-called because of the marvelous display of lights and color.

The year 1937 was an important one in the history of the Union. In that year three meetings were held: the Pan-American Education Conference in Mexico City, the Inter-American Aviation Conference in Lima, Peru, and the Inter-American Radio Conference in Havana, Cuba. In December, 1936, the Eighth International Conference of

American States was opened in Lima by the President of the United States, Franklin Delano Roosevelt.

This conference, held in Peru and attended by President Roosevelt, was important for several reasons. In order to understand why these reasons are important we must go back to the earlier years of the Pan American Union's existence.

Differences in race, languages, and customs—and in some cases religious differences—had helped to build up a feeling of aloofness between the peoples of the Central- and South-American countries and the United States. For many years there had been strained relations between Mexico and the United States. Little or nothing was done until 1889 to improve the relationships. The United States government had maintained a strangely indifferent attitude toward Pan-American conferences and its attitude of many years' standing would be difficult to break down. Writers and journalists, especially in South America, were bitter in their criticisms of the coolness of America's strongest and largest nation. Then the resolution adopted in 1930 to celebrate a Pan-American Day, together with President Hoover's significant visit to Puerto Rico, the "steppingstone between Latin America and the United States," began to create a different attitude in our sister countries.

President Roosevelt's "good neighbor policy," as set forth in his historic "Good Neighbor" speech in 1933, began to lift the curtain of doubt from the minds of the people of Latin America. When Secretary of State Cordell Hull attended the seventh Annual Pan-American Conference, and President Roosevelt opened the Lima, Peru, Conference in December, 1936, and when all United States Marines were recalled from Central- and South-American countries, then at last the other members of the Union were convinced of our friendliness. The tone of the press in the Spanish and Portuguese papers of the South American republics changed. Now they wrote without bitterness, without condemnation, with sympathy and understanding, and with buoyant hope for the future. Reserve and aloofness on both sides of the Gulf of Mexico had vanished. United States flags were flown with those of other American nations.

The Governing Board of the Pan American Union consists of the Secretary of State of the United States and the ambassadors, ministers, and chargés d'affaires in Washington of the Latin-American countries. The nineteen republics comprising the membership are as follows:

Argentina, Brazil, Chile, Colombia, Costa Rica, Dominican Republic, Ecuador, Guatemala, Haiti, Honduras, Mexico, Nicaragua, Panama, Paraguay, Peru, Salvador, the United States of America, Uruguay, and Venezuela.*

A Pan American Union Building was built in Washington in 1910 by Andrew Carnegie. It is a very beautiful edifice and is visited by hundreds of thousands annually. Its chief interest to visitors is its magnificent tropical garden in a Latin-American courtyard, where colorful flowers

* As of 1965, Bolivia and Cuba were not members.

and fountains give one a glimpse of the natural tropical beauty of the southern republics represented by this building. It is more than likely that hundreds of school children seeing this bit of Latin America have resolved to visit the countries themselves. If and when they do, a magical world of wonder awaits them! There is Mexico, land of the Aztecs, source of some of the world's finest pottery, country of color and romance; Central America, with its islands of magical splendor, fine old cities, and beautiful shores; and South America, overflowing with extravagant tropical beauty, unforgetable for its great rivers and mountains, and its wild, broad pampas.

During and since the Second World War, events have transpired that made more imperative than ever a closer cooperation among all the nations of the Pan American Union. A number of important steps were taken to bring about a stronger unity of purpose. A series of Foreign Ministers' Conferences of the Union began immediately after the outbreak of the war. After the war had ended, these conferences were mainly concerned with a security system and with the problems of a Communist threat to the Western Hemisphere.

Finally, at the Ninth Conference of American Republics, held in Bogotá, Colombia, the Organization of American States was formed. All of the twenty-one American republics signed the charter for the OAS on April 30, 1948. The purpose of OAS was, and is, to settle peacefully all disputes; deal with economic, social, and political problems of the member countries; and promote inter-American cooperation and understanding. The headquarters are in Washington, D.C., at the Pan American Union. The Pan American Union is the central and permanent organ and Secretariat of the OAS. Because the Castro regime in Cuba became a growing concern of the other American nations, in 1962, when the Consultation of Foreign Ministers met in Punta del Este, Uruguay, Cuba was expelled from the "inter-American system" and the following resolutions were passed:

That Marxism-Leninism was incompatible with the principles and objectives of the inter-American system, and

That this incompatibility excluded the present Government of Cuba from participation in the inter-American system.

At this conference, which was attended by all twenty-one American republics, United States Secretary of the Treasury C. Douglas Dillon presented President John F. Kennedy's plan for an Alliance for Progress. The plan offered $20 billion to Latin-American countries over a ten-year period with the condition that the governments receiving aid would make the necessary reforms for the economic and social development of the various nations. All the member nations with the exception of Cuba signed the Alliance for Progress Agreement.

At the first anniversary of the formation of the Alliance for Progress in 1963, President Kennedy called attention to some of the benefits thus far: slum clearances begun;

140,000 new housing units and seven hundred new water systems built; 8,200 new classrooms and four million school books put into use; more than nine million children being fed in eighteen different countries. President Kennedy pointed out that this was only a start, but plans were made for many future reforms.

The inter-American nations have a long way to go to achieve their goals, but with the impetus of the Alliance for Progress, the OAS may look forward to improving their future as never before, politically as well as in economic and social affairs. Pan-Americanism, it seems to us, has a firmer foundation than at any time in its history. As we celebrate Pan-American Day each year on April 14, may it be with the fervent hope of all Americans that real progress will continue to be made in unifying the nations of our Western Hemisphere!

May Day

MAY 1

Through many centuries and in many lands May Day has been observed with customs characteristic of the times and the people. Most of the celebrations have revolved around the Maypole. Even today, on the first day of May we see it, gaily decorated with bright streamers of ribbon and surrounded by groups of dancing children or young women, the center of a May Queen festival in our city parks or on some college campus.

An old Hungarian legend tells about the first Maypole, or May Tree as it is called in Hungary. May 1 is a Saint Day, dedicated to the Apostles St. Philip and St. James. The story goes that on a certain May Day centuries ago, a good Christian woman was walking forth with her staff in her hand when she was accosted by her enemies and accused of wrongdoing. The woman, knowing her innocence but being unable to prove it to her accusers, in desperation thrust her wooden staff into the ground and called upon the good Saints Philip and James to send some sign to prove her innocence. It is said that as soon as her prayer was uttered, her staff sprouted green leaves and twigs and became a living, growing tree. From then on the May Tree was the symbolic center of May-day observances.

Many believe that May Day had its origin with the Druids because of their worship of trees, specifically the oak, which had an important place in the rites of the ancient Druid priests. On the other hand it seems more likely that the custom of observing a festival at this time originated in ancient Rome. For here we see much similarity to the later May-day celebrations. The Roman festival was held in honor of Flora, goddess of flowers and springtime. Known as *Floralia,* it was a joyous festival lasting from April 28 to May 3. At the beautiful Temple of Flora the celebrations were most significant. By tradition, the first to place a wreath or garland at the temple was assured of good luck throughout the coming year. Ropes of flowers were twined about its marble columns, while, all around the temple and on the streets, blossoms were thrown in great profusion by children and young women who were dressed in loose robes of white and wore flowers in their hair. The *Floralia* marked the beginning of spring, and the Roman people celebrated it for several days.

The May-day festival, whether a relic of the pagan Druids, or a carry-over of the Roman *Floralia,* was to the English people of the Middle Ages the happiest of the whole calendar! Although the day has been celebrated for several hundreds of years, at no time did it assume so much importance among rural communities of England as in the Middle Ages. May Day has always been closest to the country folk, for it is, after all, a true festival of Nature. All through

the long, cold winter months the peasants looked forward to spring. And when May Day came round, spring had really arrived in fullest array, with flowers and green-growing things in wood and field. This, then, was the time of the year when country people could rejoice in the fresh new beauty of their own land and realize anew what it meant to them. Flowers were a symbol of happiness, and green-growing things were symbolic of new life and new hope for the future. It was a time of joy, of song and dance, to young and old. In every small village and rural community the people were off to the woods, returning at daybreak on May-day morn, laden down with boughs and blossoms. Thus they "brought home the May." And bringing home the May Tree was a most important part of the celebration. Historians tell us that the Maypole in some parishes of London was so huge that it took several yoke of oxen to draw it to the village. From an account of May Day in Chambers's *Book of Days* we read:

Not content with a garlanding of their brows, of their doors and windows, these merry people of the old days had in every town, or considerable district of a town, and in every village, a fixed pole as high as the mast of a vessel of a hundred tons, on which each May morning they suspended wreaths of flowers, and round which they danced in rings pretty nearly the whole day.

In some villages the Maypole was erected in front of the church, where it was believed to keep evil influences from entering. From another historian of bygone days we have a further account of the Maypole.

They have twenty or forty yoke of oxen, every ox having a sweet nosegay of flowers placed on the tip of his horns; and these oxen draw home this Maypole which is covered all over with flowers and herbs, bound round about with strings from top to the bottom, and sometimes painted with variable colours, with two or three hundred men, women and children following it with great devotion. And thus being reared up, with handkerchiefs and flags hovering on the top, they strew the ground round about, bind green boughs about it, set up summer halls, bowers and arbours hard by it, and fall they to dance about it.

The procession at early morn on May Day from the woods back to the village was gay with song and dance, jest and laughter. Jolliest of all were the morris dancers, they of the ribbons and streamers and bells at knee and toe, who performed with unceasing merriment to the great joy of the spectators. The morris dance is said to have originated centuries ago in Spain, but it has come down to us with all the character of the English folk dance. To a student of English peasant life it is characteristic of the joyous holiday spirit of the people.

In Somerset and Cornwall there was the hobbyhorse dancer. He was an oddly grotesque figure, wearing a huge mask over his head to represent a horse, and with nondescript draperies of all colors hanging down to conceal his feet. Accompanied by a drummer and an accordion player, he went through all sorts of weird and comical antics, sending his audience into raptures of delight. He must have been a fantastic-looking creature, for there is a legend that many, many years ago, the town of Padstow in Cornwall was threatened by invasion from the French, but when the invaders caught sight of the hobbyhorse they fled!

It was the custom for all good housekeepers to have their housecleaning done by the time May Day came round, and one thing necessary to a clean house was a clean chimney. In those days of huge fireplaces and gigantic chimneys, there were small urchins whose work was to climb up the chimneys with their brooms, at the bidding of their masters, and sweep out the black soot of a winter's accumulation. Tom, the chimney sweep in *The Water Babies* by Charles Kingsley, was one of these. On May Day all the chimney sweeps took part in the procession. They danced and sang and collected pennies, and a strange sight they must have been with their ragged, sooty clothes in the midst of the well-dressed villagers. But since they were to be rewarded after the parade with a dinner of roast beef and plum pudding, it is safe to wager that none missed being there! Another group in the parade was comprised of milkmaids. They paraded with their cows, and both maids and cows were festooned with ribbons and blossoms. Stagecoaches and horses were also there, trimmed all over in every place where a flower or streamer could be fastened. One extraordinary feature of every May-day parade was the "Jack-in-the-green," usually to be found with the chimney sweeps. "Jack-in-the-green" was, literally, Jack enclosed within a green bower—a light framework of wood in which he was almost completely hidden by green boughs and flowers. The frame and its occupant were carried on the shoulders of several men. Just how this feature of May-day parades originated is not known.

There were many superstitions connected with May Day. One of the most popular was that of hanging hawthorn over one's door to keep out the witches! Another practice among the girls and young women of the village was that of bathing their faces in the morning dew on May-day morn, which was believed to assure them of lovely complexions for the coming year. This custom is still followed in some parts of Scotland. In Edinburgh, the young people rise early on May Day and ascend the steep hill to "Arthur's Seat," the summit that overlooks the city. There, at sunrise, they wash their faces in the morning dew.

In Ireland, in the olden days, dew was sometimes collected and placed in bottles and applied when needed, for
it was thought to have healing powers. It was said that a
heavy dew on the first of May was the sign of a good butter
year. The Irish went to great pains to help along a good
yield of butter. Clay was removed from the split of a cow's
hoof and placed with a coal of fire and a bit of salt under the
butter churn. Then the witches were defied. Witches were
almost as conspicuous on the eve of May Day as on Halloween. "If you dare to tease the cat on this night, don't be
surprised if it turns into a witch!" One sure way for mortal
man to be able to see the old women on May Eve was to put
his clothes on wrong side out and walk backward to the
nearest crossroad—if he had the courage!

Even the ancient Romans had a superstition against
marrying in May. Said Ovid: "If you regard old saws,
mind, thus they say: 'Tis bad to marry in the month of
May." An old English maxim on this subject tells us:

Marry in May,
You'll rue the day,
To marry in May,
Is to wed povertie.

At the time of the Puritans, May Day lost much of its
popularity in England and was observed only surreptitiously
because of the ban on all such frivolities. Many or most of
the Maypoles were uprooted when Parliament in 1644 made
them unlawful. But, after the Restoration, May Day came
into its own again. Never again, however, was the holiday

so wholeheartedly celebrated as it had been before the Puritans.

Choosing a May Queen for the May-day festivities has existed since May-day celebrations had their beginning, and is one custom of this holiday that has not been lost. During the first days of May there are fairs and festivals held in towns throughout England and Scotland. Over each of these a May Queen presides. On the first Sunday following May Day there is the great London May Queen Festival held at Hayes Common, near Kent. Here are assembled all the beautiful May Queens of the lesser festivals. From these lovely girls, one is chosen "May Queen of London." She is crowned with elaborate ceremony and presides over the festival.

In some of the outlying districts of London, small children still go about on May Day carrying a doll dressed in white—the lady of the May. Going from house to house, they sing carols and give away the flowers they carry, expecting pennies in return. When there is a knock at the door and the lady of the house sees the children wreathed in smiles and holding forth small nosegays of flowers, she realizes that it is May Day and that a halfpenny is expected of her.

Although May Day seems to belong more appropriately to England than anywhere else, it is observed in other countries in various ways.*

* See Labor Day for those places where May Day is observed as a labor holiday.

In some parts of Europe, May-day Eve is known as
Walpurgis Night, and fires are kindled with great hilarity
"to burn out the witches." * In the Highlands of Scotland
Beltane Fires are lit on the hilltops. These are said to be
a relic of the ancient Druid rites. In Scotland and Ireland
today there are still the old wishing wells. A wish made at
the wishing well on May Day will surely come true! And
in Ireland it is said that if a girl sees her lover's reflection as
she makes her wish, and if it be just at sunrise on May Day,
she will be married to him before the year is out. It is said,
too, that a maid of Dublin, if she wishes to see her future
husband on the morrow, places a stocking filled with yarrow under her pillow the night before May Day. There was
a special verse to be chanted over this ritual:

> *Good morrow, good yarrow, good morrow to thee;*
> *I hope 'gain the morrow my lover to see,*
> *And that he may be married to me;*
> *The colour of his hair, and the clothes he does wear;*
> *And if he be for me may his face be turned to me;*
> *And if he be not, dark and surly may he be,*
> *And his back turned to me.*
>
> —FROM NOTES AND QUERIES

Because of the scarcity of timber in Ireland, the Maypole
has not been used there for years, although in some places

* Walpurgis was an early missionary to Germany, born in England in the
eighth century. Walpurgis Night is observed in various countries at various
times, but usually on May Eve.

the small mountain ash is brought into the village for this purpose. But everywhere on May Day there are flowers—lilacs and hawthorn, and great fields of golden gorse in fullest bloom. Primroses gathered before sunrise and strewn about the house bring good luck to that house—or, better still, a bunch tied to the cow's tail! The Irish peasant folk have many pleasant superstitions relating to May Day. On May Eve the "wee people" are very active. They play their fairy pipes and can easily be heard by those who have the courage to seek them out, although it is said that they who listen to such sweet music are not long for this earth. Many are the strange sights that have been seen on the first day of May. Enchanted cities in a mist of magic rise up from the sea in all the sparkling beauty of the past ages. It is said, too, that O'Donoghue of Killarney comes up from his castle under the waters and rides upon a snow-white steed, a retinue of lords and ladies following him.

In modern Greece the May-day fetes are celebrated with girls in traditional white robes doing the graceful, classic dances that have made Greek dancers famous for centuries. All the schools are given a holiday and practically everyone spends it in the woods, where wild flowers are gathered and fashioned into wreaths. These wreaths are taken home and hung up until the Eve of St. John, June 23, when they are burned in the great bonfires that are kindled according to tradition for that purpose.

May Day in Italy is for the most part a day of sports meets, races, and contests of all kinds. In Modena, how-

ever, the day is known as the Maytime of the Maidens, and
is a very romantic day indeed. This is the time for young
lovers to serenade their sweethearts. When a girl is sere-
naded by her swain standing beneath her window, it is a
pretty sure sign that the two will wed before the year is out.

In Switzerland the *Maitannli,* or May Pine Tree, is placed
under the sweetheart's window. They say that if a girl is
quite unpopular she may find, instead of the gaily decorated
Maitannli, an ugly straw man—a veritable scarecrow!

Huge fires are kindled in Sweden on May Eve to keep
the witches away. These fires in Stockholm, on Reindeer
Mountain, are made from great piles of logs, barrels, and
boxes, and the light from their blaze can be seen for miles
around. One of the old customs of Sweden was that of
sprinkling grass on the doorsteps to keep out the witches
who roamed on that night. The witches had to count the
blades of grass before entering, giving those inside fair
warning.

In a great many places flowers are exchanged on May
Day. In Denmark lovers exchange wreaths made from a
dried plant. In Poland boys and girls carry twigs of green
from house to house which they sell for a few cents. These
sprigs of green are supposed to bring good luck to the
house, especially to cattle and crops. The French have a
custom of exchanging *muguets*—nosegays of lilies of the
valley. Making a wish while wearing a *muguet* from a
friend is supposed to make the wish come true.

In France on May Day one sees small children collecting

pennies "for the May." One will have been chosen to represent the Virgin of the May. They dress her in a robe of white and crown her with a wreath of flowers. Then, surrounded on her throne by other little girls, she is the center of a picture which is thought to be worthy of a donation of small coins from passers-by. One very old custom in the vicinity of Paris is that of drinking May milk at dawn on May Day—milk that is still warm and foaming, fresh from the cow.

In the United States May Day has never had the same background of tradition and custom that it has enjoyed in England and other countries where it is celebrated. Whatever customs were brought to America from England in colonial times were straightway destroyed by the Puritans in New England. Nathaniel Hawthorne tells of an attempted celebration round a Maypole in Massachusetts in the early days of that colony. The governor was so enraged by the demonstration that he hacked the pole to pieces with his sword.

The May-day customs here, therefore, are those retained by early English settlers who dared to carry out the old practices and by those people from other countries who have settled in America during the past few generations. In Chicago, for instance, the Greek dances of May Day are performed by the Greek population and are fast becoming traditional. In Palo Alto, California, there has been for years a May-day festival for children.

One rather universal observance of May Day in the

United States is the fete held everywhere on college campuses throughout the country. Dancing about a Maypole with a May Queen presiding and her ladies-in-waiting in attendance is one tradition that we hope will never die. The one held at Bryn Mawr College in Pennsylvania is perhaps the most famous of all. At Wellesley College the Seniors hold a hoop-rolling contest in connection with their outdoor festival on May Day.

Quite often on the green mall of city parks and at some of the city playgrounds we see the Maypole on the first of May, with ribbon streamers and children dancing round it. With the green grass and the scent of flowers, and the sun shining down upon the youthful dancers and upon the May Queen who is crowned with flowers and wreathed in smiles at the honor bestowed upon her, the scene is not very different from those May festivities of four or five hundred years ago. It is a celebration too full of meaning and too steeped in tradition—the tradition of the ancient Roman *Floralia,* and of countless generations of English people who honored May Day, and of people everywhere who recognized the hope and joy of another spring—to be permitted to go out of existence. Let us hope that it never will!

Mother's Day

A certain Hebrew proverb says: "God could not be everywhere; therefore He made mothers." Observing a day in honor of our mothers is a comparatively new idea in this country. But for many years the people of England have had such a day. It is called Mothering Sunday. Observed on a mid-Lent Sunday, the day was kept by visiting one's mother and taking her a gift—usually a delicacy called *simnel,* cake made of finest wheat flour. An old poem from Herrick's *Hesperides* mentions it.

> *I'll to thee a Simnel bring*
> *'Gainst thou go'st a-mothering;*
> *So that when she blesseth thee,*
> *Half that blessing thou'lt give me.*

In several countries of Europe, mothers are honored on Saint Anne's Day. Saint Anne was the mother of Mary and grandmother of Jesus.

The Yugoslavs have a quaint Mother's Day—*Materitse*—when the children of a family bind up their mother and won't let her go until she has promised them something good to eat! In Serbia, a province of Yugoslavia, the mother hides little gifts under her pillow for the children.

The first suggestion for a special commemorative day in this country, so far as we know, came from the writer of that famous classic of the Civil War, "Battle Hymn of the Republic." Julia Ward Howe's idea was to establish Independence Day as a Mother's Day, making it a day of peace. The suggestion apparently was never taken seriously. Later—in 1904, at a convention of the Eagles Lodge at South Bend, Indiana—a proposal was made by one of the members, Frank E. Hering, that a day be set aside each year to honor mothers.

But the real founder of the day was Miss Anna Jarvis of Philadelphia. Wishing to honor the memory of her own mother, Miss Jarvis conceived the idea of observing a day in each year to honor mothers everywhere. To that end she worked for many years, traveling thousands of miles, making speeches, writing letters, and giving all her time and effort to the cause. Finally, after having spent two years in Washington, Miss Jarvis saw her dream realized when, on May 8, 1914, President Wilson signed a joint resolution in Congress in which he ordered that the second Sunday in

May be observed each year as Mother's Day, authorizing the display of the flag on all government buildings on that date. On that first official Mother's Day President Wilson wore a white carnation in his lapel as a mark of respect for mothers.

The custom of wearing carnations on Mother's Day is part of the story of Miss Jarvis's mother. Mrs. Anna Reeves Jarvis was the mother of eleven children, wife of a minister, and proud owner of a garden on the grounds of their home in West Virginia. Known all over town for her great kind heart, Mrs. Jarvis found real pleasure in distributing flowers to those who had none. It was because of this passion for flowers that her daughter, years later, chose one as a symbol of "the Mother of Mother's Day" and selected a carnation.

In writing about Miss Anna Jarvis in an article about "Mother of Mother's Day," Ann Hark has this to say concerning the choice of a white carnation:

The whiteness of the blossom . . . represents the purity of motherhood; the calyx symbolizes life; its fragrance is like the incense of a mother's prayers; its wide field of growth exemplifies the boundless charity of a mother's love; its enduring characteristics, her fidelity. And, crowning touch of all, the carnation's habit of folding its faded petals to its heart instead of dropping them . . . illustrates as no other picture could the undying quality of a mother's love.

In establishing the custom of Mother's Day, Miss Jarvis stressed the importance of sending a message to Mother on her day. The occasion has become commercialized to such an extent that telegrams conveying appropriate sentiments are now available at special rates. Shops, department stores, drugstores, flower shops, and other places where gifts can be bought are lavish in their displays, reminding the buyer to purchase a gift for Mother on Mother's Day. However, the day itself is heartily welcomed by individuals everywhere who want to take this special opportunity of showing gratitude to Mother.

After realizing her dream in America, Miss Jarvis turned her attention to other countries, hoping to make the day one of international observance. Her idea took root almost instantly abroad—in England, France, Sweden, Denmark, Hawaii and the Sandwich Islands, Samoa, China, Japan, India, Palestine, and other countries from one end of the globe to the other. In Mexico the holiday lasts two days.

Tree planting has been a popular feature of Mother's Day programs. On that day in Washington trees have been planted in honor of American mothers and the mothers of the Presidents of the United States. In Los Angeles there is a park called Mother's Memory Garden in which the California Mother's Tree is planted.

In honor of the day a special United States postage stamp was issued in 1934 bearing the world-famous picture of Whistler's Mother.

A great deal has been done to keep the observance of Mother's Day alive by the Golden Rule Mother's Day Committee of the Golden Rule Foundation. Every year since 1935, this committee in New York City, in addition to sponsoring essay contests on the subject of Mother's Day, has selected some woman in the United States as the typical American mother. Besides being a good homemaker and parent whose children reflect the soundness of their upbringing, she must hold an outstanding place in the civic and social life of her community.

In observing the second Sunday in May we are doing more than just showing our love for our mother. We are giving expression to a feeling of respect and reverence for all mothers everywhere—those now living and those who have passed on. Many of them have blessed the world with sons and daughters who have made great contributions to civilization. "All that I am or hope to be, I owe to my angel mother. Blessings on her memory," said Lincoln. Years later another famous American spoke thus: "My mother was the making of me," said Edison. "She was so true, so sure of me, and I felt I had someone to live for, someone I must not disappoint."

Most beloved of all famous mothers is Mary, Mother of Jesus. Gentle, loving, and pure, she symbolizes the sacredness of mother love through the ages, and we see her today wherever the spiritual light of love shines through a mother's eyes.

Your silent tents of green
  We deck with fragrant flowers;
Yours has the suffering been,
  The memory shall be ours.
—HENRY WADSWORTH LONGFELLOW

Memorial Day

MAY 30

Most countries have one day in the year set apart
for honoring the dead. Because our Memorial Day was
started immediately after the Civil War, it was, for many
years, devoted to the remembrance of those who died in that
war both in the North and in the South. But the history of
our country includes several wars since that time, and it was
only natural that those who sacrificed their lives in those
later wars should be honored on Memorial Day. In recent
years, the Congress of the United States has suggested that
Memorial Day should be celebrated not only by honoring
the dead but also by praying for peace.

Several places in the United States have claimed the honor
of being the first to observe a Memorial Day for the veterans

124

of the Civil War. Boalsburg, Pennsylvania, claims this distinction because several women on a Sunday in October, 1864, visited the cemetery of that town and decorated the new graves of soldiers who had been killed in the war. By May 30, 1869, Decoration Day, as it was called, was an established custom there. In 1964 the people of Boalsburg celebrated the one hundredth anniversary of their "founding" of Memorial Day. But meantime, two other places were also celebrating their own founding of this holiday. These were Columbus, Mississippi, and Charleston, South Carolina. In any case, the custom of decorating the graves of Civil War veterans became established in many places.

Finally, the suggestion to name a specific day was made to the National Commander of the Grand Army of the Republic, General Logan. In 1868, he named May 30 to be set aside "for the purpose of strewing with flowers or otherwise decorating the graves of comrades who died in defense of their country during the late rebellion, and with the hope that it will be kept up from year to year."

The custom *was* kept up for many years by the "comrades" and later by the organization of the Sons of Veterans of America. In 1882, the G.A.R. urged that the designation "Decoration Day" be changed to "Memorial Day." May 30 is now a legal holiday in all states except the following: Alabama, Georgia, Louisiana, Mississippi, South Carolina, and Texas. In Virginia it is known as Confederate Memorial Day. In several southern states it is observed with Jefferson Davis's Birthday on June 3, a legal holiday.

Every year just preceding Memorial Day, the task of placing a new American flag on the grave of every man and woman who served in the Armed Services of the United States is undertaken by local chapters of the American Legion, the Veterans of Foreign Wars, the AMVETS, and the Jewish and Catholic Veterans Associations. Members of these organizations volunteer each year to do this work, while other volunteers from the Sons of Veterans annually decorate the graves with flowers. In towns and cities all over the nation there are services held to honor these dead. Parades, bands, assemblies, and speeches are the order of the day. Probably the most oft-repeated speech at this time is Lincoln's Gettysburg Address, and certainly one of the most famous of the country's memorial parks is the battleground at Gettysburg.

In July, 1938, at the seventy-fifth anniversary of the Battle of Gettysburg, a celebration on the battleground was attended by eighteen hundred surviving veterans of the Civil War. Guests of the government, they came from all points in the United States. On July 2, before a gathering of 150,000 persons, President Franklin D. Roosevelt dedicated a monument on Oak Hill called the Eternal Light Peace Memorial. A Union soldier of the G.A.R. and a Confederate soldier from Georgia unveiled the shaft rising fifty feet above the ground, topped by a steadily burning flame visible for a distance of twenty miles. The inscription on the monument reads: "An enduring light to guide us in unity and fellowship."

Each year on Memorial Day the National Cemetery at Arlington, Virginia, is the scene of an impressive ceremony, as are also many other national cemeteries throughout the nation.

On public buildings and on all government ships, flags are flown at half mast until noon on Memorial Day.

There is a beautiful custom observed in all important ports of the United States on Memorial Day when those

who have died at sea are honored with a picturesque ceremony. Tiny ships laden with flowers are set afloat upon the water to honor those who have died in the service of the United States Navy.

The Saturday preceding Memorial Day is Poppy Day in most of the states and in other countries where there are veterans of the two World Wars. These tiny red artificial poppies, with a tag marked "Honor the Dead by Helping the Living," are sold under the sponsorship of Veterans of Foreign Wars, for the benefit of disabled veterans. The idea originated in France, but the poppy has become a familiar symbol in England, Canada, the United States, Australia, and New Zealand, as well.

Decorating graves is an ancient custom, having been observed by the Druids and the ancient Greeks and Romans. At the time of the *Parentalia,* the chief annual festival of the dead, the Romans placed garlands of flowers on the graves of their loved ones. Today the Italians observe All Souls', at which time prayers are said for the souls of the departed.

An ancient Chinese custom is that of Ch'ing Ming, the Festival of the Tombs, when all the people visit the cemeteries of their dead. They make this a happy occasion, for after the rituals are performed at the graves, the families spread picnics at the scene and eat the food they have brought for the spirits of the dead. Another Oriental custom is that of placing lighted candles on flat bits of wood and floating them on the waves to honor those who have died at sea.

France annually observes the *Jour des Morts* when the people carry wreaths to the graves, making the cemeteries bright with flowers. The Rumanians always celebrated a memorial day on the Eve of Trinity, when presents were given in exchange for prayers for the dead. A Memorial Day is celebrated in Finland on the third Sunday in May. In Turkey the date is August 30.

While American soldiers were still in France after World War I, there were several Memorial Day services conducted "over there." Of these, the one held at Suresnes Cemetery near Paris on May 30, 1919, was most notable. President Woodrow Wilson made the address, and in it he made an impassioned plea to all countries to join the League of Nations. The dream of his heart, that of seeing the United States become a member, never materialized. "It is for us," he said in that address, "particularly for us who are civilized, to use our proper weapons of counsel and agreement to see to it that there never is such a war again."

We know that his desires and hopes for world peace were not realized. Since his time, the League of Nations functioned for some years, and after World War II the United Nations was formed. Perhaps the United Nations is the instrument for peace that Wilson had envisioned in his hopeful look into the future. When the graves of men killed in battle have at last become only a historical memory, then indeed will Memorial Day be a time of dedication and rededication to the causes of peace, not only for our own country but for all nations of the world.

Children's Day

There are several days of the calendar that might be called Children's Day. First of all there is a Children's Day observed in most Protestant churches. Started by the Methodist Episcopal Church in June, 1868, when the custom began to be observed annually, it was gradually adopted by other churches. On the second Sunday in June the church service is given over to the Sunday school. In some churches the children march into the church from their Sunday school rooms and every class is represented in special Children's Day exercises.

Another and much older children's church festival is Childermas, observed in Greek, Roman, and Anglican

churches. The name Childermas for the day also known as the Feast of the Innocents is taken from the account of the massacre of children in the time of Herod. Here is the account from the Book of Matthew: "Then Herod, when he saw that he was mocked of the wise men, was exceeding wroth, and sent forth, and slew all the children that were in Bethlehem, and in all the coasts thereof, from two years old and under, according to the time which he had diligently inquired of the wise men." Childermas—December 28—is considered an unlucky day on the calendar. There was a time in England when it was certainly unlucky for boys and girls, for that day was chosen to flog the children to make them good! The Puritans of the early New England colonies apparently held the same belief, for a writer of that period tells us: "It hath been a custom to whip up the children on Holy Innocents' Day morning, that the memories of this murther might stick the closer." On the other hand, a custom of Belgium made the Festival of the Innocents a happy day for youngsters, for the parents allowed them on that day to do almost anything they pleased and, furthermore, to give orders to their elders instead of receiving them!

The "Day of Innocent Martyr Saints" is observed in Mexico (December 28) in a way that is somewhat reminiscent of April Fools' Day. There the children have a custom of fooling members of their family, or the neighbors, by borrowing something of value, such as small sums of money or some prized possession, and instead of returning it, re-

placing it with some worthless trinket. The invaluable substitute in this strange custom is accompanied by a note
which reminds the victim of the trick and that they never
should have lent anything on the *Dia de los Inocentes!*

The Feast of St. Sava is a glad day for the children of
Serbia—a holiday that is looked forward to all the year. St.
Sava was a king's son who died January 14, 1236, and since
that time January 14 has been kept as Children's Day in
Serbia in commemoration of the good work St. Sava did
for children. After celebrations in the schools in honor of
the man who built schools, churches, and monasteries all
over Serbia, the day ends with feasting, music, and dancing.

Dechivi Dan is the Children's Day of Yugoslavia when
the children are tied up by their parents and not set free
until they promise to be good all the rest of the year!

December 21, or St. Thomas's Day, is observed in Belgium by a peculiar custom. The boys and girls are put out
of the house and the doors are locked. Then the older members of the family call to them through the window: "St.
Thomas's Day! St. Thomas's Day! What will you give to
come in?" And the children must pay a forfeit to get back
into the house.

April 23 is Children's Day in Turkey, and the children
have a wonderful time. Gifts of ice cream and candy are
given to them, while in Ankara the President presents a
group of school children with small gifts. The boys and
girls take over civic offices for the day. All this is done to

celebrate the anniversary of the inauguration of the Grand National Assembly on April 23, 1923.

Iceland celebrates a Children's Day on April 24, and there is one in Sweden in September.

The Festival of Dolls in Japan is a very old holiday, and an important one in that country, for the Japanese consider that the doll plays a very important role in the happiness of their children. The festival, according to our calendar, comes about the end of April. All the little girls fondly display their dolls, many of them receive new ones on this day, and all the dolls in Japan are feted! Early in June there is a day called the Burial of the Broken Dolls when, with great ceremony, all the dolls that are too badly broken to be mended are buried with Buddhist rites with real priests officiating. After the little girls have placed their dolls, some without arms and legs, some with heads missing, into the one big grave, they sing the "Song of the Broken Dolls" and seem far from sad. Perhaps they know that by the time the Doll Festival comes round they will have new dolls.

A new holiday in Japan is "Children's Protection Day," started in 1922 after the modern calendar had been accepted by the nation. Observed annually on April 17, it is a day commemorating the passing of a legal enactment for caring for juvenile delinquents. This law provides that, instead of being sent to court and to houses of detention, the boys and girls who have proven to be delinquent are placed under the supervision of chosen schools for proper guidance.

The United States now celebrates a very important Children's Day, on the first Monday in October, proclaimed annually by the President as Child Health Day. Although New York had a Child Health Bureau as early as 1908, and other cities soon afterward, the work was dropped during World War I. However, after the war the American Child Health Association urged its reorganization. Sponsored also by the Children's Bureau of the United States Department of Labor, and by the Departments of Education in the various states, Child Health Day became a successful reality. The first observance of the day was in 1924. In 1928 a Congressional resolution was adopted stating "That May 1st shall hereafter be designated and known as May Day Child Health Day and that it shall be the duty of the President to request its observance as provided in this resolution." The date was later changed because it conflicted with Loyalty Day. Congress passed a resolution to the effect that, beginning with January 1, 1960, Child Health Day would be observed on the first Monday in October.

The day is especially celebrated in the schools, with exercises and prize contests for essays on the subject of health. One very satisfying result of these years of making the public conscious of child health is the fact that health is now taught in the schools all the year round, and is not reserved simply for one special day of the year.

*I pledge allegiance to the flag of the
United States of America and to the
Republic for which it stands,
one nation under God, indivisible,
with liberty and justice for all.*

Flag Day

JUNE 14

For many years this pledge to the American flag has been repeated by millions of school children and other citizens in their salute to the flag. Written by James B. Upham, of the *Youth's Companion* magazine staff, it first came into prominence at the World's Columbian Exposition in Chicago, in 1892. And now, standing at attention, right hand over the heart, we repeat that solemn pledge, giving allegiance to the flag that protects us. Why should we pledge allegiance to a flag, a bit of decorated bunting on a stick? What does it mean? Everyone knows, of course, that the flag is a symbol of our country. It has come to mean so much to us through the years since its adoption by the nation in 1777—so much more than just a banner—that the Stars and Stripes as it waves in the breeze seems to us the soul and spirit of the land we love.

Appropriate to our love and respect for our flag, we observe Flag Day, honoring the Stars and Stripes.

The history of our flag begins with the history of our country as a nation. In 1775 the Continental Congress appointed a committee for the purpose of choosing a flag, this committee comprising Benjamin Franklin, Thomas Lynch, and Benjamin Harrison. The result was that on June 14, 1777, the following resolution was adopted by Congress: "*Resolved,* That the flag of the United States be thirteen stripes, alternate red and white, that the 'Union' be thirteen stars, white in a blue field, representing a new constellation."

There have been several reasons advanced as to why red, white, and blue were chosen for the American flag. In studying the types of flags that were in use at that time we can see that there were probably a number of factors that influenced our choice. Some historians have pointed out that the colors were chosen because the white signified purity and innocence; the red, hardiness and valor; the blue, perseverance, vigilance, and justice. Granting that, there were reasons why stripes were chosen, and stars in a blue field. It is certain that prior to 1777 there was no one flag that could be called the Union flag. It is said, for instance, that in New York in 1775 "A Union flag with a red field was hoisted at New York upon the liberty-pole, bearing the in-

scription, 'George Rex, and the Liberties of America.' "
Another flag was described by a London magazine of 1776:
"The colors of the American fleet were striped upon the
Union, with thirteen strokes, called the United Colonies,
d their standard, a rattlesnake; motto—'Don't tread on
" Another flag that was popular with the colonies was
the Pine Tree Flag. On it were the words "An appeal to
Heaven."

In 1775 the Philadelphia Light Horse Company was using a flag with alternate blue and silver stripes in the upper
left-hand corner. The following year another flag appeared
which represented the union of the colonies. From the
British Annual Register of 1776 this flag is referred to as
follows: "They [the colonies] are said to have changed
their colors from a plain red ground, which they had hith-
erto used, to a flag with thirteen stripes, as a symbol of the
number and union of the colonies." Elsewhere this flag is
described as having a blue field containing the Cross of St.
George and St. Andrew. One thing is certain, that red and
white were chosen because they had been used by the colonies in the flag of England. The blue was probably used
because it was a background for the stars "representing a
new constellation" and because blue was a popular color in
the American colonies.

We have on record these words from George Washington concerning the new nation's flag: "We take the star
from Heaven, the red from our mother country, separating
it by white stripes, thus showing that we have separated

from her, and the white stripes shall go down to posterity representing liberty."

It is believed that a five-pointed star was chosen to grace the blue field of our flag because it was used by our allies, France and Holland, while the six-pointed star was used by England.

Thirteen stripes were chosen, as were the thirteen stars, to represent the thirteen colonies that had become states. When new states were added to the Union, a new problem presented itself, and so a change was made. In 1795 two new stars were added to the blue field, and two new stripes, these representing Vermont and Kentucky. Until 1812 this fifteen-stars and fifteen-stripes arrangement was the national flag. Then five new states were added—Tennessee, Ohio, Louisiana, Indiana, and Mississippi. Should a new stripe and a new star be added to the flag for each of these states?

In 1818 Congress enacted a new law concerning the national flag.

Section 1. . . . That from and after the fourth day of July next, the flag of the United States be thirteen horizontal stripes, alternate red and white; that the Union have twenty stars, white in a blue field.

Section 2. . . . That on the admisssion of every new state into the Union one star be added to the Union of the flag, and that such addition shall take effect on the Fourth of July next succeeding such admission.

140

In studying the history of the American flag, it is not until the year 1870 that we find any mention of Betsy Ross as the maker of the first American flag. In that year the seamstress's grandson told the story that is now familiar to nearly everyone, of how George Washington, accompanied by Robert Morris and George Ross, called upon Mrs. Ross, a widow residing at 239 Arch Street in Philadelphia, and asked her to make the newly adopted flag. It is said that she was shown the design and agreed to make the flag, and that with her scissors she cut them a five-pointed star, showing Mr. Washington how it would look on the flag. Although there is no documentary evidence to support the Betsy Ross story, it is a legend that has been accepted by the American people, and Betsy Ross's name is synonymous with the making of the American flag. Her home on Arch Street is a shrine in Philadelphia that has been visited by hundreds of thousands since the Betsy Ross Memorial Association was founded in 1898. The house was purchased in 1905.

The United States is probably the only nation whose national anthem is written about the flag, although it was 117 years after the song had been written that "The Star-Spangled Banner" was officially accepted as the American national anthem. Congress was hesitant about making it official. This may have been because "My Country 'Tis of Thee" was more popular in some sections of the country, particularly in the New England states. Chiefly through the efforts of the National Star-Spangled Banner Commission, organized in 1914 on the one hundredth anniversary of

the writing of the song, it was officially accepted in an act of Congress on March 4, 1931.

It was the flag flown from Fort McHenry during the War of 1812 that inspired Francis Scott Key to write his immortal song. That flag, measuring thirty by forty feet, is now in the Smithsonian Institution's Museum of History and Technology in Washington, D.C. Frayed with age, and with one star cut from the blue field, it remains a mute reminder of that night of battle.

On the night of September 13, 1814, Francis Scott Key had obtained permission to go to the British fleet in the harbor to plead for the pardon of a friend of his family, who was being held prisoner on some minor charge. He reached the British ship safely and was successful in obtaining the pardon. Getting away was a different matter, however, for suddenly the bombardment of Fort McHenry began, and Key was forced to stay on the British ship. When dawn broke and he could see the American flag waving, he knew that the fort was still in the hands of his countrymen. It was then he wrote the song, on the back of an old envelope, calling it "The Defense of Fort McHenry." Later it was printed and distributed to stir up patriotism, and soon afterward, the war having been won, it became a popular song of victory.

There are several versions of "The Star-Spangled Banner" because Scott is said to have made some changes in various transcriptions of his song when he wrote them out for his friends. The one in the possession of the Maryland Historical Association is thought to be closest to his original draft made on the British ship.

The first Flag Day in America was observed on June 14, 1877. That year Congress requested that the flag be flown from all public buildings to commemorate the one hundredth birthday of the American flag. In 1894 a Flag Day Association was formed in Chicago. The association selected the third Saturday in June as Flag Day, but two years later the date was changed back to June 14, the actual anniversary of the day the American flag was adopted. From that time, cities and public officials observed the day, and soon it began to be celebrated in the schools.

On August 3, 1949, President Harry S. Truman signed a bill stating that "the President each year shall call for the national observance of this day."

Today school children are taught not only the history of their flag but also the formalities concerning it, or "flag etiquette." It is unlawful to desecrate the American flag in any way, and no true citizen would willfully do such a thing. There are definite formalities to be observed in showing proper respect to the flag. At a National Flag Conference held in Washington on Flag Day in 1923, a flag code was drawn up, a code which is too long to include in this chapter.

The saying that "the sun never sets on the American flag" is true. From Alaska to the Virgin Islands, the Stars and Stripes waves proudly, a symbol of the land of the free.

"Our flag carries American ideas, American history, and American feelings. Beginning with the Colonies and coming down to our time, in its sacred heraldry, in its glorious insignia, it has gathered and stored chiefly this supreme idea—divine right of liberty in man. Every color means liberty, every thread means liberty, every form of star and beam or stripe of light means liberty; not lawlessness, not license, but organized, institutional liberty—liberty through law, and law for liberty." Thus a great American preacher, Henry Ward Beecher, wrote of the Stars and Stripes of America.

Flag "Firsts"

☆ First salute accorded the Stars and Stripes by another nation was by France when Captain John Paul Jones shipped at a French port on the *Ranger*, February 14, 1778.

☆ Stars and Stripes was first admitted on equality with flags of other nations on September 3, 1783.

145

☆ First American flag to fly over a schoolhouse was in 1812, at the small log schoolhouse in Catamount Hills, Massachusetts.

☆ First Flag Day observance was June 14, 1877.

☆ First Flag Day observed by schools was in the Philadelphia Public Schools in 1893.

☆ First Flag Day Association was formed in Chicago in 1894.

☆ First National Conference on the display and respect of the flag met on Flag Day in Washington in 1919.

Independence Day

JULY 4

The Fourth of July, a legal holiday in all the fifty states, the District of Columbia, and all territories and possessions of the United States of America, commemorates the birth of a great nation.

On June 28, 1776, the Declaration of Independence, having been drawn up by Thomas Jefferson, was presented to Congress and was adopted on July 4. But it was not until August 2 that all the fifty-six signers had placed their names on the copy of the Declaration which had been engrossed on parchment. With courage, and faith in their right to freedom, the colonies severed their relations with Britain by engaging in a war that gave them their independence. The colonies became the United States of America, a republic that was to grow rapidly and magnificently into one of the greatest nations of the world.

"We, therefore, the Representatives of the United States of America," the final paragraph of the Declaration of Independence reads: "in General Congress, Assembled, appealing to the Supreme Judge of the world for the rectitude of our intentions, do, in the Name, and by authority of the good People of these Colonies, solemnly publish and declare, That these United Colonies are, and of Right ought to be, Free and Independent States: that they are Absolved from all Allegiance to the British Crown, and that all political connections between them and the State of Great Britain is and ought to be totally dissolved: and that as Free and Independent States, they have full Power to levy War, conclude Peace, contract Alliances, establish Commerce, and to do all other Acts and Things which Independent States may of right do. And for the support of this Declaration, with a firm reliance on the protection of Divine Providence, we mutually pledge to each other our Lives, our Fortunes, and our sacred Honor."

The birthday of any nation should be the proudest holiday of that nation! No country in history has had more reason to be proud of its beginning than our own. Born of the desire for freedom, nurtured by faith and courage, founded on the highest principles and ideals conceivable to man, it has faced and fought wars and civil strife, economic depressions and political vicissitudes, to emerge rich

and resourceful, mighty in the world and glorious as a nation. Nowhere else in the world have individuals the freedom and opportunity that belong to an American citizen. Richard Henry Lee had declared, in a resolution presented to Congress: "that these United Colonies are, and of right ought to be, free and independent states." That aspiration fought and won freedom for the people in the colonies and that precious heritage was given to us and to all future Americans.

The first celebration of Independence Day centered, naturally enough, in the city of Philadelphia where the Declaration was signed the year before. Philadelphia was then the capital of the nation. Regardless of the fact that war was going on, there was a hearty celebration on that first birthday of national independence. Congress gave a dinner to military officers and the city fathers, bands played, and all the city was gay with bunting, even to the ships in the harbor. Already the prophecy of John Adams was coming true. In a letter to his wife the year before, when the Declaration was accepted by Congress, he had expressed his belief in the importance of the day. "I am apt to believe that it will be celebrated by succeeding generations as the great anniversary festival," he wrote. "It ought to be commemorated as the day of deliverance, by solemn acts of devotion to God Almighty. It ought to be solemnized with pomp and parade, with shows, games, sports, guns, bells, bonfires, and illuminations from one end of this continent to the other, from this time forward evermore." Philadelphia, at least, and probably many other towns of the new nation, observed the day through the years of the Revolution and from then on to the present time. In the year 1826 Independence Day was celebrated as usual, but sadness was mingled with the rejoicing, for that day saw the death of two of the most famous signers of the Declaration of Independence, Thomas Jefferson and John Adams.

The peak of Independence Day celebrations in Philadelphia was in 1876 at the Centennial Exposition. Many nations of the world participated in the event. People from all parts of America came to celebrate the one hundredth anniversary of the nation in the city of its birthplace. It was there that Alexander Graham Bell introduced his new invention, the telephone.

One phase of Fourth of July celebrations has passed out of existence—the practice of setting off explosive fireworks. In former years Independence Day was always celebrated with plenty of noise—bands and parades, gun- and cannon-firing, and fireworks of all kinds. Every year the day was marked by the death or injury of thousands of people. At the beginning of the twentieth century the peril was at its height. As early as 1907 the fatalities for July 4 from fireworks amounted to more than 1100 persons, with twice that many injured. After protests were made and people were warned each year of the danger, the casualties dropped somewhat, but still on July 5 each year the newspapers all over the country carried stories of dead and injured. Now there are laws restricting the sale of fireworks in more than twenty states and in most cities, while some states forbid the sale of fireworks entirely. Eventually, it is hoped, all states will adopt similar measures to safeguard life and property. With the passing of firecrackers Independence Day has taken on a new character. The holiday has assumed a more peaceful mien, and more attention is given the patriotic aspects of the nation's birthday.

In Lititz, Pennsylvania, the Fourth has been celebrated since the year 1818 with a Feast of Candles. Handmade candles of every conceivable size and shape, thousands of them, are lighted in the park after darkness has fallen. Later, the crowds who have come to enjoy the spectacular sight are treated to a display of fireworks.

In 1918 Independence Day was observed in England for the first time. This observance, by the British, of a day commemorating the severance of the American colonies from the mother country marked an epoch in the amicable relations of these two English-speaking nations. England at that time had many American soldiers on her soil, while others were fighting side by side with Britain's sons in the trenches across the Channel. On this day of July 4, 1918, the Star-Spangled Banner flew with the Union Jack, and American soldiers were feted with luncheons and banquets. Most important of the functions on that day were the Meeting of Fellowship held in London at Westminster Cathedral and a baseball game between American Army and Navy men, the latter attended by George V, King of England. The Fellowship Meeting was addressed by Lord Bryce, former

Ambassador to United States—the man who, it was said, had done more than any other to cement a firm and inviolate bond between the two nations. Another speaker was Winston Churchill, who took as his text the American Declaration of Independence! From the meeting a cablegram was sent to President Wilson and the people of the United States, expressing "Heartfelt greetings on the 142nd anniversary of the Declaration of American Independence."

The American nation had come a long way since that memorable year of 1776. But the common ties of blood and language had kept America and England in close relationship, and bitterness had long since disappeared.

America's Independence Day for several generations has been observed in the north of Denmark. In Jutland, in the only park of its kind in the world, a festival is given over to the celebration of July 4. Rebild National Park was built by Danish-born Americans, and in 1912 they began the annual Rebildfest with thousands attending. After the ringing of a replica of the Liberty Bell, the United States and Danish flags are hoisted and the national anthems are sung. Programs of speeches and music follow. Other Scandinavian countries are beginning to hold similar celebrations, recognizing the freedom that is expressed by America's Independence Day.

Many nations of the world have their own independence days. The Fourteenth of July, or Bastille Day, in France, is the birthday of the French Republic. Here is a nation whose independence was won, like America's, because of a love of liberty and freedom. That Republic is similar to ours in age, in form of government, and in the character of its freedom-loving people. On the day of the *Fête Nationale* the figure of Liberty is often displayed with the French flag, reminding us of the French gift to America, the Statue of Liberty, which stands in New York harbor.

India celebrates August 15, the anniversary of her independence from British rule in 1947, as her independence day.

In Canada, there is Dominion Day in observance of the union of several separate provinces of the Dominion of Canada, by act of Parliament in 1867, into one unified dominion.

No person willingly gives up his right to liberty. We in America have been fortunate indeed, for we are accustomed to freedom—freedom of speech, freedom of the press, freedom to worship as we please. It has been so directed by our Constitutional Fathers, who said: "We hold these truths to be self-evident, that all men are created equal, that they are endowed by their Creator with certain unalienable Rights, that among these are Life, Liberty and the pursuit of Happiness."

Many speeches have been made on this famous paragraph of the Declaration of Independence. In school we study the Declaration, on the Fourth of July we observe its birth, and every day we enjoy its far-reaching results. But let us not take for granted our liberty and our right to happiness. As citizens of these United States—begun as thirteen brave little colonies, united with one purpose—let us, too, adhere to the ideals from which these states have sprung. By patriotic loyalty to all those principles bequeathed to us we can add to the greatness of America and her place in the world.

Columbus Day

OCTOBER 12

On a street in Genoa, Italy, there stands a house bearing an inscription on a tablet which, when translated, reads: *No house is more to be honored than this where Christopher Columbus spent his early youth.* It is said that in various accounts of the life of Columbus, sixteen different towns in Italy have been mentioned as his birthplace, although the general belief until very recently has been that the birthplace of the discoverer of America was Genoa. However, in 1930 the famous bibliophile Dr. A. S. W. Rosenbach brought a four-hundred-year-old manuscript to this country from London that is believed to have been written by a friend of Columbus. It gives his birthplace as Milan.

156

Cristoforo Colombo, as he was named, was born during the Renaissance in 1451. He learned the trade of weaving, but when he was fourteen years of age he ran away to sea. On returning home he tried to content himself with helping his father, Domenico. However, after a time he again followed his true love, the sea, that great uncharted world of water which to most people in those days represented only mystery and fear. When still a young boy, Christopher had read the *Travels of Marco Polo* with consuming interest and curiosity, and now that he was grown the dream of his life was to experience for himself some of the daring and colorful adventures of the Venetian traveler—a dream that was realized far more fully than the young boy could have imagined possible. The name of Columbus was destined to become one of the most famous of all time.

In the year 1470 Columbus found himself in Portugal, after his ship had been wrecked there, making navigation charts and maps to support his wife and children. But while occupied in the process of making a living, Columbus was dreaming his dream. The brilliant navigator hoped to find a short route to India, which would revolutionize trade in the Far East. In spite of the fact that he was practically alone in his conviction, Columbus was sure that the earth was round, and he intended to navigate the high seas until he found a route. He wanted to make his dream come true, but he needed money. After having tried and failed to find financial support in his native Italy and in Portugal, he went to Spain, where after many disappointments he gained the wholehearted support of Queen Isabella. Through her, he won the financial backing of King Ferdinand for the momentous voyages that were eventually to add a whole hemisphere to the known world.

On August 3, 1492, Columbus set out with three small ships, the *Santa Maria,* the *Niña,* and the *Pinta,* and a com-

pany of 120 men! On this first voyage into a new world
Columbus after four perilous weeks sighted land on October
12, the day now commemorated as Columbus Day. Although he named the land on which they set foot San
Salvador, it was what we know as Watling Island, one of
the Bahamas. He claimed this land for Spain and, believing it to be a part of India, he returned to Spain where he
was greeted with all the honor due a famous traveler.
Ferdinand and Isabella were elated. They had entertained
little hope that Columbus would be so successful. They, too,
believed that the land Columbus had discovered was India,
and that the brown-skinned men Columbus had brought
back for them to see were Indians.

Columbus made three voyages after that. On the second
voyage he discovered Puerto Rico, the Virgin Islands, and
Jamaica; on the third he touched upon the shores of South
America; but on the fourth he met with little success, either
on the voyage or on his return. Then his expeditions were
over, for almost immediately after his return to Spain from
the last voyage, Queen Isabella died. With the Queen of
Spain gone, Columbus fared ill at the hands of the country
for which he had claimed the New World. Not only did he
never receive any further recognition, but his claims to
property rights, which had been promised him, were de-
nied. Lonely, bitter, and disillusioned, Columbus died three
years after Isabella on May 20, 1506. He died believing that
the land he had found was a short route to the East. Little

did he dream that he had played the role of discoverer of America, a twin continent containing untold riches and the promise of mighty nations of the future!

As with the exact town of his birth, there is some uncertainty concerning the place of Columbus's burial. He had asked to be buried in the spot he loved best, "Española"— or Santo Domingo—in the land of his discovery. But as there was no one who cared to carry out Columbus's last wish when he died, he was buried in Seville. However, in 1542 his body, with that of his son, was sent to Santo Domingo as he had so fervently wished. The bodies of father and son were placed in the tombs of the cathedral where they remained undisturbed until the year 1795, when the Spanish island became a French possession. Spain obtained permission from the French government to remove them to Cuba, and a coffin was sent to Havana, *supposedly* containing the remains of Columbus. Then in 1877, while the Santo Domingo Cathedral was being repaired, an ancient and crumbling casket was found. On it there was an inscription: *"Discoverer of America—First Admiral,"* while on the inside lid was found further proof of its identity: *"Illustrious and noble man, Don Cristobal Colon."* * Naturally enough, the people of Santo Domingo believed this to be the original casket of Columbus, as it presumably was. Therefore, at the four hundredth anniversary of Co-

* Spanish for Columbus.

lumbus's discovery of America in 1892, a very handsome monument was erected in the ancient cathedral. Each year on the tenth of September, the anniversary of the finding of the casket, the sides of the giant urn containing the casket were let down so that visitors might see the original coffin in which the famous explorer was laid to rest. This custom was to be enacted annually until 1942 on the four hundred and fiftieth anniversary of the discovery. Meanwhile, in the cathedral at Seville, people visit "the Tomb of Columbus" to which his body was purported to have been removed from Havana. Consequently, two cities claim the honor of being the burying place of Columbus.

There are many monuments and memorials in the New World erected to its discoverer. One is the small stone shaft on little Watling Island in the Bahama group of the British West Indies. Its inscription reads: *"On this spot Christopher Columbus first set foot on the soil of the New World."*

Although the continents of the New World were not named for Christopher Columbus, there are cities, towns, rivers, and universities honoring his name. Our nation's capital, the District of Columbia, bears his name. Columbus Circle, in New York, where a fine monument stands at the Fifty-ninth Street entrance to Central Park, and the statue erected in Fairmount Park in Philadelphia in 1876 are only a few of the numerous tributes in his honor. One of the most useful of Columbus memorials is in the Pan American Building in Washington—the Columbus Memorial Library comprising the largest collection of source material and official documents on the twenty-one American republics in the world.

Columbus Day was celebrated as a holiday for the first time in 1792 in New York City, on the occasion of the three hundredth anniversary of the landing of Columbus on American soil. One hundred years later there was a national celebration followed by the Columbian Exposition in Chicago. In 1910 Boston honored October 12, Massachusetts having made Columbus Day a legal holiday that year. Through the efforts of the Knights of Columbus the day was observed pretty generally throughout the United States and in many South- and Central-American countries as well. Columbus Day is now a legal holiday in thirty-seven states and Puerto Rico. In Wisconsin it is called Landing Day.

Columbus Day parades and banquets are held annually in New York City and San Francisco. In New York, the profits from the huge banquet are donated to city students in high schools for college scholarships.

In recent years the Central- and South-American republics have almost all celebrated Columbus Day. It is also observed in Haiti, Mexico, and Canada. For a number of years Spain celebrated Columbus Day in conjunction with Racial Feast Day on October 12.

On August 3, 1951, the Trans-World Airlines made a "comparison flight" from Madrid to New York to commemorate the 459th anniversary of Columbus's voyage in

1492. The voyage of Columbus from Palos, Spain, to San Salvador in the Bahamas took seventy days. The TWA flight in the Constellation *Star of Christopher Columbus* took about thirty-one hours.

In 1492, when Columbus sighted land and imagined he had discovered a new way to India, he could not have conceived of the immensity of the land he had found! Had he been able to look ahead some four hundred years he might have seen twenty-one republics and great territories inhabited by hundreds of millions of people; great cities, vast agricultural lands, and huge forests; earth abounding in rich minerals; and great rivers, mountains, lakes, and seas— the most beautiful and productive continents on the face of the earth. Columbus's achievement, like his dreams, reached out beyond all bounds—far, far beyond the world as it was when in "fourteen hundred ninety-two, Columbus sailed the ocean blue."

Halloween

OCTOBER 31

There are still some people, they say, who believe in ghosts! If you have ever been to a Halloween party on a dark night, where the scene has been set for attracting spirits and goblins, and have walked along black corridors to an equally dark room and felt every second that icy fingers were about to reach for you, and eerie sounds made cold chills go up and down your back—well then, perhaps you, *too,* have believed in ghosts! And it wasn't a very happy feeling. Years and years ago, back in the time when Halloween began, most people did believe in spirits and ghosts, as well as in witches, fairies, elves, goblins, brownies, leprechauns, knockers, pookas, and bogies! And that was probably not a very comfortable feeling either.

In those days it kept the people very busy indeed around the time of Halloween to keep away the witches and all the other scary creatures! In Wales they used to say that "On November Eve there is a bogy on every stile." In Scotland a cautious farmer always carried torches about the fields "widdershins" (backward) in order to scare the witches from his property and save his crops. For had he not been told that all the wicked auld dames on that night turned to witches and rode broomsticks and sported with the devil? It was best to take no chances. Meanwhile the children of Scotland carried jack-o'-lanterns to protect themselves, not unlike our own pumpkin lanterns except that these were made from turnips and were called "bogies."

Burning torches and lanterns and bonfires were, and are still, appropriate to the observance of Halloween. In Wales, where hilltop fires were an important feature of this night, people gathered round and carefully tended the fires until midnight. Then, when the last red flames had turned to gray ashes, there was a mad scramble to get down the hill. And woe to the man who was last, for it was said that the devil would get the hindmost!

But how did these customs, so closely bound to Halloween, originate? What was the beginning of this holiday?

The observance of Halloween took the place of several very old holidays, and it has been kept alive these many years because it was celebrated at a popular time of year for festivals. Most peoples of ancient times observed certain festivals at the turn of the seasons. The Celts and Druids of

Ancient Britain, before the invasion of the Romans, had three important ones. These were observed on May 1, June 21, and November 1. This last was known as Summer's End, or *Samhain,* pronounced *Sah'win.* It marked also the death of the old year, for the Druid calendar celebrated November 1 as the beginning of the New Year. The Druids believed that on the day of *Samhain* all the souls of the dead who had not lived good lives on earth would be compelled to enter into the bodies of animals, while those who deserved it would be given souls of humans. There were many cruel religious rites performed by the Druid priests at this festival of *Samhain,* some of which historians have traced back as far as the Cult of Dionysus of ancient Greece.

With the invasion of Britain by the Romans the Celtic customs, with their heathen and ofttimes unspeakably cruel rites, were changed. A new influence crept into the observance of *Samhain.* It was no longer called *Samhain,* but *Halligan,* and then All Hallows. When gradually the *eve* of All Hallows came to be the time of celebration, that day was called Halloween. The invaders' observance of this day was in honor of the Roman festival *Feralia* which came at the end of October. *Feralia* was a religious day in Rome given over to praying for the dead, and especially honoring those heroes of Rome who had died for their country. This influence, and the Druidistic belief in reincarnation that was supposed to take place around this time, very likely have given Halloween the atmosphere as we know it today—of ghosts and spirits and the supernatural.

166

The custom of kindling fires came from the Druid priests and their sacred fires built at their crude stone altars. To the pagans, fire was a symbol of immortality. There has been a belief among all primitive peoples for centuries that fire will frighten away evil spirits, and this probably was the reason for bonfires and torches and the hilltop fires of Halloween.

For hundreds of years in a town in Somerset, England, the children have paraded the streets on the last Thursday in October carrying small candle lanterns made from mangels, or beets. They call them "punkies."

There is an old Irish legend concerning the origin of jack-o'-lanterns: because of his stinginess, a man named Jack was kept out of heaven and was not allowed to enter hell because of the jokes he played on the devil. His only recourse was to roam the earth, and he was condemned to do just that until Judgment Day, carrying a lantern.

The popular custom of telling fortunes on Halloween probably came from the fact that this was the Celtic New Year, and the first day of the new year has always been considered a good time to tell fortunes. The Irish and Scots had all sorts of ways of foretelling the future. Many of these dealt with a girl's finding out who her husband was to be. If she made a cake of flour, salt, and soot, ate it, and went to bed, the man who came to her in her dream offering her a drink of water was the man she was to marry! Another method was to throw a ball of yarn into the outside bake oven. Holding fast to one end, the girl was supposed to wind it in slowly until she felt it being held by someone (supposedly her true love), then she would call, "Wha'hauds?" And if she were lucky, the name of her future husband would come into her from the kiln-pot. A good way for a man to see his future mate was to sow hempseed.

> *Hempseed, I saw thee,*
> *Hempseed, I saw thee;*
> *And her that is to be my true love,*
> *Come after me and pou* thee.*

Throwing apple parings over the left shoulder is still done on Halloween today as it was then, swinging the unbroken paring over the head three times before it drops to spell the initial of the beloved.

Nuts are used in many places to foretell the future on Halloween. Indeed, in some parts of northern England Halloween has been called Nutcrack Night. Parties gather before the fire on this chill autumn night to tell stories—tales of ghosts probably—prognosticating the future with the nuts as they roast them. Those that burn bright upon being thrown into the fire supposedly bring good luck and prosperity to the person who threw them. If a young man and a maid each throw a nut into the flame and they burn together, that means the two will be married!

In England, girls used to pick yarrow and put it under

* pull

their pillows hoping to see the vision of their future husbands in their dreams; while a youth who wanted to know the identity of his future wife could put nine grains of oats in his mouth and walk abroad until he heard her name spoken!

A description of the activities of an Irish household on Halloween in the early nineteenth century gives us an idea of the importance of the old customs to all members of the family.

The buxom good wife was regaling her friends with merry lamb's-wool [punch] while her lively children and their young guests indulged in the usual superstitions and quaint customs of All Hallow Eve. Three of the eldest lasses were lurking in a dark corner busily employed in kneading a cake with their left thumbs. Not a sound escaped from their clenched lips; the work proceeded in mute solemnity; a single word would have broken the charm and destroyed their ardent hopes of beholding their future husbands in their dreams after having partaken of the mystic "dumb-cake."

Halloween in Ireland, even to this day, is celebrated by a dinner with special foods not served at any other time of the year. The writer just quoted tells of a Halloween dinner consisting of "laughing potatoes," turkey, colcannon, and apple pies. The colcannon was a very special Halloween dish made from mashed potatoes, parsnips, and chopped onions into which had been placed the following: *a ring,* designating marriage; *a doll,* predicting children to come;

a thimble, meaning the recipient would be an old maid;
and *a coin,* standing for wealth. Today this same custom is
often carried out at Halloween parties, the objects for foretelling the future of those who receive them being baked in
a cake.

Cabbages have played a role in Halloween customs on
the British Isles. In Scotland young women traditionally
determined the appearance of the men they would marry by
drawing, blindfolded, cabbages from the garden. A close
white head meant an old husband, while an open green
head meant a young man! Then his disposition could be
determined by the sweetness of the stem's taste. It was said
that a cabbage hung over the door would give a much better

clue to the man's identity, for the first man's name spoken by anyone who entered would be the Christian name of the future husband! Children placed cabbages before the door, believing that a baby sister or brother would come to the house before the year was out.

It was bad luck to eat blackberries or sloes on *any* day except Halloween, or so it was believed in some sections of England.

There was so much superstition connected with the happenings of Halloween in old Scotland that a child born on that day was said to have supernatural powers. As Sir Walter Scott pointed out in *The Monastery,* "It's weel kenn'd she was born on Halloween whiles see mair than ither folk."

Halloween in the time of Queen Elizabeth I was a real holiday, with shops closed and lots of parties, fireworks, and parades. Even as long ago as that there was ducking for apples at parties, and other Halloween games were played that are familiar to us today.

The custom of masquerading on Halloween probably came down to us from mummers in the English parades and guisers in Scotland who dressed in queer costumes and went about chanting rhymes. Today in Scotland it is the children who are guisers. They dress up and go from house to house carrying their lanterns made from large, scooped-out turnips in which a candle glows. "Anything for the guiser?" they ask at each house, as American children ask, "Trick-or-treat?"

Boys and young men of Syria dress up in funny clothes and go from house to house on Halloween, pretty much as we do here in America, and they are received with cakes and a special drink flavored with anise.

In modern Ireland on Halloween people eat sowens—

porridge made from the husks of oatmeal—and also barm-brack, a kind of bread containing raisins and currants. Colcannon is still eaten there, too, as the feature dish of a Halloween meal.

While Halloween in America lacks the superstitious character of the Old World holiday, it does, nevertheless, retain many of the old customs, such as masquerading, visiting from house to house, bobbing for apples, and eating the ever-popular apples and nuts of the autumn season. It is now chiefly a holiday for the children, though grown people like to entertain on Halloween, too. School parties are the custom now, especially for the children of the lower grades, and on the afternoon of Halloween in the average American town strange little people can be seen on their way home—little Indians and Chinese and gypsies—carrying a small orange-colored packet of nuts and candy corn, and perhaps an apple from the class party.

A recent custom in the United States is that of collecting coins for UNICEF during the week of Halloween. Young volunteers spend hours ringing doorbells and asking for "something for UNICEF children," and many thousands of dollars are raised in this effort to help the underprivileged children of the world through the United Nations Children's Fund.

The decoration of store windows is another recent Halloween innovation. In more and more towns every year, stores are giving over their large display windows to school children for picture painting contests. Armed with poster paint, which wipes off easily after the holiday is over, the children vie with each other in the artistry of depicting their favorite Halloween subjects—goblins and ghosts, witches riding their broomsticks, moons, and graveyards, and hoot owls!

In many towns there are Halloween parades for school children, with prizes offered for the best costumes. But aside from the parades and parties, Halloween night is a great occasion for the children, for it gives them freedom for fun and pranks that no other holiday permits. If a gate disappears on Halloween and is found next day hanging from the branch of a tree, that was the witches at their tricks! If the doorbell rings or there is a *tick-tack* at the window, it's spooks! And there's the fun of being disguised so that even the next-door neighbor has a hard time recognizing these odd-looking people who have come to the front door—to say nothing of the ginger cookies, apples, pears, nuts, popcorn, peanuts, and candy that disappear like magic every time they are passed round! In the olden days this may have been an important holiday for grownups, but today it is a time for the boys and girls, one of the happiest holidays of the whole year and one not likely soon to disappear.

All Saints'
and All Souls'

Halloween—Allhallows Even—is the Eve of All Saints' Day, and its celebration in some countries coincides with the customs of that holy day. November 2 is All Souls' Day and some customs of the three successive days have much in common. Since the origin of Halloween was the Roman *Feralia,* a time for praying for the dead, and All Souls' is a day devoted to that purpose, there is at least a slight similarity between the two days. In Wales, the Eve of All Saints' (Halloween) is spent in telling fortunes, trying to determine the future; while twenty-four hours later on the Eve of All Souls' the minds of the people have turned to the dead. On the Eve of all Saints' the peasants of Wales used to believe that they could, by peeping through the keyhole of the church door, see the apparitions of those who would pass on to the next world in the year to come. On the Eve of All Souls' they were praying for the souls of those who had already departed. There and in some parts of England they have at this time what they call a soul-cake, because in years gone by it was customary to give a cake in return for prayers for the dead.

> *Soul! Soul! for a soul-cake!*
> *I pray, good misses, a soul-cake!*
> *An apple or pear, a plum or a cherry,*
> *Any good thing to make us merry,*
> *One for Peter, two for Paul,*
> *Three for Him who made us all.*

So the carolers sang on the Eve of All Souls' as they went about from farmhouse to farmhouse, "souling." Because soul-cakes were thought to bring good fortune, some people kept them in the house from year to year. In Yorkshire All Souls' Eve was known as Cake Night, for it was the custom there for the mother of the family to bake a special seed cake for every member of the family.

Portuguese children on All Souls' receive sugar-cakes made of herbs, sugar, and cinnamon as a reward for their songs.

In France there is a combined celebration of All Saints'

and All Souls'. On the day before All Saints'—Halloween —children go about begging flowers to put in the cemeteries. There is a very distinct difference, however, in the celebration of the two days. On All Saints' there are flowers and lighted candles in the churches, and the music is that of rejoicing. But on All Souls' the atmosphere changes to one of great solemnity. Draped with black, the church assumes a funereal aspect. The French are very respectful of the dead on All Souls'; the cemeteries are crowded with men, women, and children who are busy decorating the graves of their departed.

In Belgium, All Souls' Day is celebrated with candlelight processions, and there is an old Polish belief that the Lord comes to the cemeteries on All Souls' to count the souls of those fortunate ones who have been saved.

Many European people not only decorate the graves with flowers and wreaths but also leave gifts there for the souls of the dead. In Lithuania, great baskets of food are taken to the cemetery, where the people partake of the feast of good things, leaving for the departed the food that was not eaten by the living!

The Mexicans observe a three-day All Souls', from October 30 to November 2. The last day is the Day of the Dead, and from sunrise until the end of the day the cemeteries are crowded. There, too, great amounts of food are carried to the cemetery, and a good time is had by all, for the Mexicans make a holiday of this day and devote it to the children, those living and those departed. Among the eatables there is always "Dead Men's Bread," candied pumpkin and chocolate, and sweets made in the shape of skulls and coffins! The celebrators always remember to leave behind them sweets for the dead.

Chinese and Japanese calendars include a festival corresponding to the occidental All Souls'. In China it is called the Festival of the Unforgotten Dead; in Japan it is the Feast of Lanterns, celebrated from July 13 to 15. After the souls have feasted for a period of three days they are content to pass on to the world beyond, and are lighted on their way by lanterns.

All Saints' Day in our own country is observed in the Roman Catholic and Protestant Episcopal churches. In the State of Louisiana it is a legal holiday. The Roman Catholic churches also observe All Souls' Day.

Veterans Day

formerly Armistice Day

NOVEMBER 11

Eleven o'clock on the eleventh day of the eleventh month in 1918—that was the beginning of Armistice Day, now a legal holiday in the United States in all states but Wisconsin. Since 1945 it has been known as Veterans Day or, in a few exceptional places, Victory Day. The original holiday commemorated the Armistice ending the First World War after four years of terrific struggle—1914 to 1918—in which almost every nation of the world had become involved. For three days in the Forest of Compiègne, a peace treaty had been discussed between Marshal Foch and representatives of the despairing German government.

179

At last the terms were agreed upon, and at five o'clock in the morning the Armistice was signed, with orders for all hostilities to cease at eleven A.M. that day.

The first Armistice Day in America, in the British Isles, in Italy, and especially in France where most of the fighting had taken place, was a day of untold joy! Peace had come— peace at last, after four awful years of unspeakable fighting on land, in the air, and at sea. Peace! All that mattered was the cessation of fighting, the silence on the battlefields, the emptying of the trenches, the crowds thronging the streets, and every heart overflowing with gladness! As the bells rang out and whistles blew and people shouted and wept and sang for joy, a new holiday was born. What the day was to mean in the future was no concern at this time of precious victory.

On the night of the Armistice, crowds grew dense as the streets of European cities, darkened for so long, once more blazed with lights. In Paris the cafés overflowed with people who wished to stay up all night to discuss the wonderful turn of events. In London thousands of people pushed their way to Number 10 Downing Street and sang, "Lloyd George, Lloyd George, oh, he's a jolly good fellow"—while twenty thousand people pressed, singing and cheering, against the palace, where the Royal Family came out upon the balcony to rejoice with them. In New York crowds went wild; bands played; a tremendous shower of paper littered the streets and fell like snow upon thousands of hysterically happy Americans. This was the first Armistice Day.

The first anniversary of the Armistice, in 1919, found the world still in the throes of reconstruction and rehabilitation after the chaos of battle, with innumerable problems, international and internal, that would take years to solve.

The following year Armistice Day was observed in France and in England by the impressive ceremony of the burial of an Unknown Soldier by both nations. France disinterred an unidentified *poilu* from among her 1,357,800 dead, placing him with reverence and sadness in a sarcophagus in the *Arc de Triomphe,* Paris. A perpetual flame burning there since that time honors the one who represents all of the French soldiers who fell in World War I.

On that same day in London a similar ceremony took place at famous Westminster Abbey. From the graves of nearly one million men Britain honored one—an Unknown Soldier—as the symbol of all who had given their lives for their country. Thus another famous tomb took its place in the Abbey among a legion of English kings and queens. For one week after November 11 the grave was left open while thousands filed by in an almost continuous line. On the day that the tomb was closed a maple leaf arrived from a Canadian comrade who had fought for the Motherland, and it was placed in the sarcophagus of the Unknown Soldier.

Following the custom of France and England, America buried her Unknown Soldier on the next Armistice Day, November 11, 1921. There were four American cemeteries in France filled with white crosses, marking the last resting places of thousands of our men who had crossed the sea and

fought valiantly at the front, only to perish. In the National Cemetery at Arlington thousands more lay buried. From France an American soldier was to be brought to Arlington, one of the many whose graves were marked *Unknown*. Because of the cruelty of war many soldiers had necessarily to be buried without ever having been identified. The United States would choose one of these nameless lads to symbolize the American youths who had fallen.

From each of the American cemeteries—Belleau, Bony, Romagne, and Thiancourt—a body was disinterred. The four coffins were taken to the City Hall in Châlons-sur-Marne and placed in a flag-draped room. Then, while the band played the sad notes of a funeral dirge, a sergeant of the Fifty-ninth Infantry placed a bouquet of white roses on one of the four coffins. The coffin upon which the white roses lay was placed in a casket marked with this inscription: *"An unknown American soldier who gave his life in the great war."*

In this manner was the identity of the soldier concealed. Arriving in Washington on November 9, the body remained lying in state in the rotunda of the Capitol Building, for three days. The steady stream of mourners passing by testified to the respect and reverence of the American people. On Armistice Day countless wreaths were placed about the casket. From all over the nation and from many foreign countries came flowers and messages. From King George V of Britain, written by his own hand, came these words:

"As unknown and yet well known, as dying, and behold, we live."

Armistice Day was officially made a holiday the year the Unknown Soldier was buried. President Harding and Secretary of War Weeks were the speakers at the ceremony at Arlington. On that day in England, General Pershing had decorated the grave of the British Unknown Soldier at Westminster Abbey with the American Congressional Medal of Honor.

Until 1938 Armistice Day was a national holiday by annual proclamation of the President of the United States. On June 4, 1926, a Resolution in Congress had provided "That the President of the United States is requested to issue a proclamation calling upon the officials to display the flag of the United States on all Government buildings on November 11th and inviting the people of the United States to observe the day in schools and churches, or other suitable places, with appropriate ceremonies expressive of our gratitude for peace and our desire for the continuance of friendly relations with all other peoples." Then by an act of Congress approved May 13, 1938, Armistice Day was made a legal holiday "to be dedicated to the cause of world peace. . . . Whereas, It is fitting at this time of world unrest that November 11, 1938, the twentieth anniversary of the armistice, should be observed with suitable ceremonies manifesting our belief that peace can be attained only by nonaggression and can be made enduring only by respect for the rights of others and good will among the nations of the world."

In 1954, by an act of Congress, Armistice Day became Veterans Day, and since that time it has been observed to honor veterans of the First and Second World Wars and the Korean conflict.

In churches throughout the United States the Sunday preceding Veterans Day is dedicated to peace, honoring the heroes of the nation's wars. At eleven o'clock on the morning of November 11, a two-minute silence is observed by people attending ceremonies here in America and also in England. England and France have observed this day for many years. In England and in Canada it is called Remembrance Day. Belgium, too, holds Armistice Day ceremonies, notably in the city of Brussels.

184

At the ceremony at Arlington National Cemetery each year on Veterans Day, a wreath is placed at the Tomb of the Unknown Soldier by the President of the United States.

Whether we call it Veterans Day, Armistice Day, or Remembrance Day, this is truly a day for remembrance. In honoring the men and women who have sacrificed themselves for our country, it is our solemn obligation to remember not only the victories of war but all its untold horrors and suffering as well. Times have changed since the two World Wars. Atomic weapons have created the greatest menace to civilization that mankind has yet known. May we all, as citizens of the world, look upon that menace as a great challenge, for in military victory there is defeat, but in peace there is a possibility of victory.

Thanksgiving Day

FOURTH THURSDAY IN NOVEMBER

"Over the river and through the woods, to Grandmother's house we go!" That's the song they used to sing on Thanksgiving Day, and that is what they used to do. Nearly everyone who had grandparents went to their house for a big family gathering on Thanksgiving Day and—more important to the children—a big family dinner. Turkey, cranberry sauce, mashed turnips and giblet gravy, pumpkin pies and apples and nuts—plenty of everything! The song goes: "The horse knows the way to carry the sleigh o'er the white and drifting snow!" Bells were jangling, children were shouting from the straw-filled body of the sleigh, and blankets were pulled up to chins by mittened hands as

186

father guided the horses with mother beside him, anxious to arrive in time to help with the big dinner. Then there was the fun of unloading, rushing to get into the warm kitchen where the odors of a delicious feast were almost overpowering to hungry senses! To describe the way the turkey tasted, that browned, handsome bird just bursting with chestnut filling and so big that he covered Grandma's huge white platter from edge to edge, would only be doing an injustice to the turkey!

Let us go back to the first Thanksgiving Day in America.

It was the year 1621 and the date was December 13. That day had been set in the Plymouth Colony by Governor Bradford as a time for being thankful and showing gratitude to Almighty God for the bounties received in this land of hardship and struggle. Elder Brewster conducted the Thanksgiving church service among the loyal band of fifty-five in the Plymouth settlement. Then there was a rare feast for these people who had perforce to be very sparing with food. Governor Bradford had appointed four of the best marksmen to go hunting and bring back enough food for a feast. They had been unusually successful, having brought back to the settlement many wild turkeys and quails. The Pilgrims were joined at their feast by King Massasoit and ninety Indian braves who presented Governor Bradford with the welcome gift of five deer. History tells us that this first Thanksgiving lasted for three days.

It is quite probable that the idea for a Thanksgiving Day presented itself to the Pilgrims through any one or all of three sources. First, the English had, in the course of history, observed various days of thanksgiving from time to time. Guy Fawkes Day in that country had originally been a day of thanks proclaimed "in grateful deliverance" after the uncovering of the famous Gunpowder Plot in 1605—a plot to blow up Parliament on November 5 of that year, discovered in time to avert the disaster. Although Guy Fawkes Day was dropped from the British calendar in 1833, it is still observed to some degree in England, Australia, and some other territories. Other days of Thanksgiving, proclaimed by the ruling monarchs of England and set aside as days of gratitude for some victory or other, had been observed from time to time.

Another influence that cannot be ignored came from Holland. It will be remembered that the Pilgrims, after fleeing from England, had found refuge with the Dutch for several years before deciding to brave the hardships they later encountered on the wild, strange shores of America. The men, women, and children so earnestly seeking religious freedom were happy in Holland, and while making their homes with the peace-loving Hollanders they probably acquired the custom of observing their holidays. In Holland there was a Thanksgiving Day in October in remembrance of Holland's victory over Spain in the year 1575.

The third possibility as a reminder to the Pilgrims to establish a Thanksgiving Day was the influence of the Indians. King Massasoit was friendly toward the Pilgrim Fathers and it is not hard to imagine that the Indian custom

188

of celebrating "thanksgiving" days appealed to the devout
founders of New England. From histories of the American
Indians and their customs we know that most if not all of
the tribes observed times of thanksgiving.

Because of the boisterous type of celebration in vogue at

that time, Christmas was condemned as sinful and its celebration was absolutely forbidden in the New England colonies, but Thanksgiving was faithfully observed. A law was passed to the effect that a fine of five shillings be imposed on those who did any "servile labour or worke" on Thanksgiving Day.

But the American Thanksgiving had no established permanence as a holiday for more than two hundred years after its first celebration. During the Revolution there were eight different days of Thanksgiving appointed by the Continental Congress as days of gratefulness for victorious battles in the war. The first move to set aside a national holiday in which the whole country might take part did not come until 1789, when President Washington designated November 26 of that year as a national Thanksgiving Day. But unity, even in the matter of holidays, was difficult at that time, transportation and communication being what they were. After 1795 there wasn't another national Thanksgiving Day until 1862, when Abraham Lincoln called on the nation to give thanks for victories in the Civil War.

And now we come to the great defender and initiator of our official Thanksgiving Day, Mrs. Sarah Hale. Editor of *Godey's Lady's Book,* Mrs. Hale worked for many years for a Thanksgiving that should be a truly national holiday— equal in importance to the Fourth of July! This sincere and persevering woman made herself personally responsible for seeing that *all* the states should observe the day. She wrote to the governors urging their support, and thousands of letters from her pen went to those who could help along the cause. She sent President Lincoln a copy of George Washington's proclamation in which he had asked the people to observe the day (November 26, 1789) "to the service of that Great and Glorious Being Who is the beneficent author of all the good that was, that is, or that will be."

Her reward came when President Lincoln's proclamation in 1864 made the last Thursday in November an annual national holiday. Today Thanksgiving is a legal holiday in every state, territory, and possession of the United States. The custom since Lincoln's time, by tradition, has been for the President to proclaim the holiday for the District of Columbia and the territories and possessions of the United States, and for the governors of the states to follow suit by proclaiming the holiday for their respective states. On the Sunday preceding Thanksgiving Day, the President's proclamation is read from pulpits in churches all over the nation.

In his proclamation of August 15, 1939, President Franklin D. Roosevelt called upon the nation to observe Thanksgiving on the third Thursday in November in 1939 and 1940, a deviation from the usual custom. It was felt that a longer shopping period between the Thanksgiving and Christmas holidays would result in an increase in business. However, beginning with 1941, by a ruling of Congress, the traditional fourth Thursday was made a legal holiday.

Thanksgiving Day is probably more of a family holiday than any other on our calendar. It is a time when all who can possibly do so go home. Schools and colleges usually give students a vacation of several days. In every town and city in America there are early morning church services, and in a great many places there are important football games.

Children in some cities dress up—paint themselves like Indians or mask as they do on Halloween—and beg pennies from people on the street. In New York City it is not unusual to be approached by costumed children with a frank plea for pennies. "Anything for Thanksgiving?" they ask. This custom is thought to be a relic of the old British Guy Fawkes Day.

In certain sections of Pennsylvania there is a sect known as the Schwenkfelders—so-called from their founder, Kaspar von Schwenkfeld, a German follower of John Huss in the early sixteenth century—who have a Thanksgiving Day peculiar to themselves on September 24. It commemorates their landing in Philadelphia in 1724, when they came to this country seeking religious liberty as the Pilgrim Fathers had done a hundred years earlier.

Since ancient times there have been holidays and festivals similar to our Thanksgiving. Among the Israelites certain feast days were set apart for giving thanks. The Greeks celebrated nine days of thanksgiving for the harvest in their Feast of Demeter. Its counterpart was the Feast of *Cerelia* in Rome. The Druids of Ancient Britain observed a harvest festival in November, while the early English Harvest Home was an important time of the year among the country people.

The Scots celebrate the Kern, when the harvest is taken in. In late September there used to be harvest festivals among the Czechoslovakians, Poles, and Lithuanians, while in Russia the harvest festival was one of the most important of the whole year. Famous at the festival of the Russians was the *khorovod,* a dance expressing the entire routine of the harvest. At that time a wreath from the year before, made from wheat, oats, barley, and rye, was removed from the side of the house with customary ritual, and a new one was put in its place while the girls and boys chanted, "Good luck, good luck to the house."

In Yugoslavia, Harvest Home festivals featuring dancing in native costume are held in August.

"Harvest Thanksgiving" is celebrated in Austria in the month of October.

A harvest feast called *Höst Gilde* is celebrated in Norway when the harvest has been taken in for the year.

The Siamese have a "Swing Festival" which is observed annually to show gratitude for bounties received.

In Canada, Thanksgiving Day is celebrated each year, usually on the last Thursday of October.

Returning once more to the first Thanksgiving Day in America, it may seem strange to us now, living on this continent in the midst of all the comforts the Pilgrims lacked, that they who fought every hardship for existence should have found something to be thankful for. But the Pilgrim Fathers were grateful for the same things for which the Indians thanked their gods—tall, waving corn in the fields;

pumpkins on the vine; potatoes; turkey; deer; the sunshine and rain that brought the harvest; and the forests that yielded wood for protection and warmth. If they could be thankful for the bare necessities of life, we who have so much have good cause to celebrate Thanksgiving Day. And while being grateful, let us not forget those patient, persistent, hard-headed colonists, who braved the uncivilized world of a new continent to establish a land of freedom for their children, their children's children, and for you and me.

194

And she brought forth her first-born son, and wrapped him in swaddling clothes, and laid him in a manger; because there was no room for them in the inn.

And there were in the same country shepherds abiding in the field, keeping watch over their flock by night.

And, lo, the angel of the Lord came upon them, and the glory of the Lord shone round about them: and they were sore afraid.

And the angel said unto them, Fear not: for, behold, I bring you good tidings of great joy, which shall be to all people.

For unto you is born this day in the city of David a Saviour, which is Christ the Lord.

—ST. LUKE 2:7–11

Christmas

DECEMBER 25

In the little town of Bethlehem, Judea, birthplace of David the king, Jesus was born of Mary nearly two thousand years ago. That was the first Christmas.

There is no other day of the year like Christmas. In every Christian country of the world it is the most important and meaningful holiday of the whole calendar year. Commemorative of the birth of Christ, it is also the anniversary of a new age, the era of Christianity. For on that day there came into the world a Great Teacher who was to bring light to countless millions, influencing whole nations and races of men. His birth is celebrated annually from one end of the

195

world to the other in churches and great cathedrals, and in the homes and hearts of the people.

Strangely enough, the date of Christ's birth is not known with certainty. As a matter of fact, it was not until 354 years after His birth that December 25 was first observed as His birthday. Some believed the true date to be November 17; others claimed it was March 28. But since the year 354 when Bishop Liberius of Rome started to observe Christmas on December 25, that date has been accepted by Western Christendom.

Although the true meaning of Christmas is its religious observance, there are customs associated with this holiday's celebration that have been grafted on from pagan times— ancient customs that survived the age in which they were born through continuous practice by the people. The *Saturnalia* of Ancient Rome made its contribution, and customs were borrowed from the Druids of Western Europe and Celtic Britain, from the Ancient Germans, and from Scandinavia and Persia. Either directly or indirectly, the Roman, Persian, Norse, Hebrew, Gothic, and Anglo-Saxon worlds lent their influence to the celebration of Christ's Birthday.

It is true that for many years the holy day was kept as a church festival only, with reverent ceremonies in early Christian churches and none of the outside influences just mentioned. But as Christianity spread, its holidays and holy days were celebrated with intense enthusiasm and according to native taste by the peasant classes of England, Ireland,

Scotland, and many nations of the continent. Those were the days when May Day was at its height in Merrie England, and Halloween in Ireland and Scotland was an important occasion. From the distinctly religious character of Christmas, the pendulum swung the other way, and in the early seventeenth century the holiday became so rowdy and boisterous that it was abolished by law! This was during the time of the Puritans, for, with their wholly restrained way of living, they frowned upon all holidays, considering them worldly and frivolous. In 1643, while the Puritans were in power, Parliament abolished Christmas, Easter, and Whitsuntide from the calendar and made their recognition unlawful. Likewise, in the New England colonies of America, the Puritan influence was being felt. In the Massachusetts Bay Colony a law was passed making the observance of Christmas a penal offense. That was in 1659 and the result was rather sad for New England, for this prejudice was so deeply imbedded in the minds of the stern Pilgrim Fathers that more than a hundred years passed before the day was celebrated to any extent. About the time of the Civil War Massachusetts began to observe some of the Christmas traditions of the rest of the country.

Prior to the "relapse" which the holiday suffered at the time of the Puritans, there were years of joyful Christmas celebrations in England that form a part of English tradition. The first keeping of Christmas on record in England was in the year 521 when King Arthur took over the city of York with a real celebration there in the truly Christian manner, banishing heathen rites that reflected the still-persistent Roman *Saturnalia*. From an ancient book published in 1608 there is an account of Christmas as it was celebrated by a certain rich squire of the time, showing that period's enthusiasm for the holiday:

At a Christmas time, when great logs furnish the hall fire—when brawne is in season, and, indeede, all reveling is regarded, this gallant knight kept open house for all commers, where beefe, beere, and bread was no niggard. Amongst all the pleasures provided, a noyse of minstrells and a Lincolnshire bagpipe was prepared—the minstrells for the great chamber, the bagpipe for the hall—the minstrells to serve up the knights meate, and the bagpipe for the common dauncing.

Minstrels were used in the court of the king. Those mentioned above were probably wandering minstrels, a group of men who traveled from place to place making music, and of course at Christmas time they were more than welcome in the big houses that overflowed with guests and the joyful spirit of the season! Known as the Christmas waites, there were usually four or five men who carried bagpipes and drum, or fiddle, flageolet and harp, which they employed with plenty of vigor in all the tunes they knew. Celebrations were not confined to one or two days. In the great houses of the country squires they were apt to last from Christmas to Candlemas, a period of five weeks. From Christmas to Twelfth Night was a time of continuous feasting, music and dancing, frolicking and fun—a veritable carnival. It was about this time that the Lord of Misrule came into being; at this time, too, that Christmas lost its religious character and at the same time fell out of favor with the Puritans.

The Lord of Misrule was a strange stepchild of Christmas, seeming to us, as to the Puritans of that time, far removed in spirit from the celebration of Christ's birthday. In the time of Elizabeth I the Lord of Misrule was at the height of his popularity. Chosen by the people to head the Christmas festivities, he in turn chose a Fool and a Jester as his two chief assistants. These three made plans for the celebrations, heading the Mummers and planning the parades. Misrule it was, for law and order were forgotten by the noisy, boisterous, lawless crowd that took possession of the town at this time. All the true significance of Christmas was lost in that queer unrestrained way of celebrating. We cannot wonder at the Puritans' abhorrence of the day.

In spite of this period when the holiday for a time ceased to be celebrated, England was to find Christmas once more. Years later a famous English writer was to make the English Yuletide world-famous. Charles Dickens's immortal *Christmas Carol* is probably more familiar to the world today than any other Christmas literature with the exception of the story of the Nativity.

Today no holiday on the calendar is so dear to the heart of an Englishman as Christmas. The English children hang up their stockings just as the American children do. The house is decorated with holly and mistletoe from Christmas

to Candlemas, and of course there is always a Christmas tree! In England, the tree is often kept in a tub of earth so that it may be replanted, a custom that is just beginning to be adopted elsewhere as much better than letting the evergreen wither and die and be thrown on the ash heap—the tragedy of Andersen's "Fir-Tree." The idea of a living Christmas tree seems more in keeping with the Yuletide spirit.

What would Christmas be without a Santa Claus? That indispensable and genial character who *is* Christmas to

200

millions of little children all over the world has come into being through tradition that has grown with the centuries. His story is an interesting one. Yes, indeed, there *was* a real Santa Claus!

St. Nicholas, or *San Nicholaus* as it is pronounced in several foreign tongues, of which Santa Claus is a contraction, was a saint whose feast day is December 6. That is why in Holland and Belgium December 6 is the day when boys and girls receive their gifts from him instead of on Christmas Day.

Nicholas was born at the close of the third century in Lycia, Asia Minor. Later he became Bishop of Myra and gained distinction as a member of the Council of Nicea, in the year 325. The good bishop was famed for his kind heart. A story is told of his helping three maidens who were without suitors. It is said that he filled three purses with gold and threw them into the homes of the young women, and soon after, with such dowries, they were married. After that, any unexpected gift was attributed to Nicholas. Gradually, through the years, he came to be known as the patron saint of children. In the town of Bari, Italy, where St. Nicholas is buried, he is not associated with Christmas. His day is celebrated there not in December but on May 7, because that was the day, in 1087, on which his remains were brought from Asia Minor and buried at Bari. Pilgrimages are made to the beautiful temple built there in his honor.

St. Nicholas seems to have been adopted first by Holland as the patron saint of Christmas. Today, in some form, his name is familiar to children of nations scattered over the entire world. True, he is not always known as St. Nicholas or even as Santa Claus, but he is nonetheless real to the children for all that. Father Christmas, *Kris Kringle, Pelznickel, Yule Tomten, La Befana, Petit Noël, Christkindli*— each of these is Santa Claus to the little ones of some land, and extremely important to a Christmas celebration.

The legend that Santa Claus comes down the chimney belongs to the Norsemen. They had a goddess Hertha, who appeared in the fireplace to bring good fortune to the house. From them also came the custom of burning the Yule log. The *Juul* was burnt annually in honor of the god Thor. So well established had the custom become that in England, in the days of Christmas waites, boar's head dinners, and mutton pies, the Yule log was the most important feature of the occasion. With a great deal of ceremony it was brought in and placed in the huge fireplace in the great center hall where the fire was started with a bit of the old Yule log from the year before. The English still have their Yule log. In Serbia, great importance was always attached to the burning of the *Badnyak* and to certain significant rituals that were thought to bring good fortune to the house.

The giving of gifts at the Christmas season is reminiscent of the Wise Men who brought gifts to the Holy Child: "And when they were come into the house, they saw the young child with Mary his mother, and fell down, and worshipped him: and when they had opened their treasures, they presented unto him gifts; gold, and frankincense, and myrrh."

In France, instead of hanging up their stockings, the boys and girls put out their shoes for the *Petit Jesu* to fill. This custom started long ago when children placed their shoes, filled with oats, on the doorstep for the camels of the three Wise Men that they might eat while on their journey to Bethlehem. If they had been good children they found that the Wise Men had left gifts in their shoes. In Spain, Mexico, and Latin-American countries, children place their shoes at the foot of the bed or on the balcony on the Eve of Epiphany, January 6, for that is the time the Wise Men are supposed to have come to visit the Christ Child.

One of the most beautiful customs of the Birthday of Christ is the representation of the Nativity story. From the most ceremonious rituals on midnight of Christmas Eve in the world's largest and most beautiful cathedral, St. Peter's in Rome, where the Pope with his Guard of Honor and the Bishops and Cardinals take part, down to the tiniest minature Bethlehem arranged under a Christmas tree, all are evocative of that holy night when Christ was born. In an Italian household there is the *Presepio,* dear to the heart of every member of the family. *Presepio* is the Italian word for stable, but it is now used to designate the scene of the Nativity, with its shepherds, camels and sheep, the three Wise Men, the figures of Mary and Joseph, and a little manger containing the tiny figure of the *Bambino,* the Holy

Infant. In our own country we have a custom of arranging little villages, with trees and houses and people, under the Christmas tree. The Moravians of Pennsylvania have their *Putz* at Christmas. The *Putz* is similar to the Italian *Presepio* except that it is always under or near a tree with a bright star suspended above it. Some of the scenes occupy half a room. The tiny figures of the *Putz* are saved from year to year and for generations, cherished by the family that owns them. A moss-covered hillside on which sheep are grazing, a tiny shepherd looking up at the bright star, and, in a sequestered part of the hillside, a cavelike stable holding its precious burden, with Mary and Joseph nearby and the three Wise Men kneeling at the door—all these create an impression of realism to the beholder. The first *Putz* this writer ever saw was in Nazareth, Pennsylvania—a scene such as has just been described. The only light in the room came from the gleaming star hanging above, and as visitors looked down on the little Judean scene, the mother of that household related in soft tones the story of the First Christmas.

Every Christmas season in Mexico brings the *Posadas,* an enactment of the Nativity that lasts for nine nights. Nine families take part, and each night the group meets in a different house. A procession starts the *Posada,* led by two children carrying images of Mary and Joseph. Followed by family, guests, and servants, they wander from room to room chanting the Litany of Loretto. At the door of each room they beg for admittance and are refused. But in the last room they are admitted, and here there is an altar representing the scene of the Nativity with tiny figures and an empty manger in the stable. On the first night the figures of Mary and Joseph are placed in the stable, but the manger remains empty until the last *Posada* on Christmas Eve.

In Christian homes in Iraq, there is a custom of burning

dried thorns in the courtyard of the home after the Christmas story has been read from the Bible. Great emphasis is placed on the manner in which the thorns burn, since this is supposed to foretell the fortune of the house for the coming year. A psalm is sung while the fire is burning, and when the fire is out everybody jumps over the ashes and makes a wish.

What would Christmas be without music? The custom of having music at Christmas began in the churches hundreds of years ago, in the form of litanies. Today every church prepares special Christmas music. Relics of the old-time English waites are the carolers who sing outside the houses Christmas Eve or early Christmas morning. Anyone who has ever awakened at dawn on Christmas to hear voices of men and women ringing through the clear, cold air in some beautiful old carol such as "O Little Town of Bethlehem," or "Silent Night," will agree that it is a custom well worth keeping. The major part of Christmas for the Ukrainians—observed by them on January 7—used to be spent in singing carols. Groups of young *kolyakniki* went from house to house singing hymns in praise of the Christ.

In Rumania it was the custom for boys to carry bags with them on their caroling to receive the gifts that were given to them. Singers in Poland used to carry a star around with them. Sometimes they dressed themselves to represent characters of the Nativity story.

In Spain, where the weather is warm on Christmas Day and the whole world seems filled with flowers and music, there is dancing, for when the Spanish people are happy, they dance.

Every nation that celebrates Christmas seems to have some special dish for the Christmas feast. Long ago in Merrie England, boar's head and brawne, peacock and mutton pies seemed essential to a successful Yule dinner. These mutton pies were a forerunner of our own mincemeat pies. In Scotland it was the custom for some member of the family to rise before any of the others and prepare breakfast, which had to be eaten in bed. Bannocks, oaten cakes, were baked on the griddle for every member of the family. It was believed to be unlucky if any of these broke in the baking.

Christmas cakes are popular in every country. The Moravians here in America are famous for their thin-as-paper, temptingly delicious Christmas cakes, made in all sizes and shapes weeks before Christmas. *Pfefferküchen,* hard spice cookies, are popular in Germany. In Denmark the thousands of tiny cakes baked for Christmas consumption are known as pepper nuts.

The wafers that the Polish people make for Christmas, *oplatki,* are stamped with representative religious figures and blessed by the priests. Then they are given away as gifts, and even used as Christmas cards. These wafers also are objects of a ritual performed among Polish families on Christmas Eve. When the first star appears in the Christmas sky, each member of the family breaks the *oplatki* for another, while solemn greetings are exchanged.

Turté, a special bread or cake, the dough of which is

supposed to represent the swaddling clothes of the Infant Jesus, are eaten in Rumania. The Serbian Christmas cake, called *chestnitsa,* contains a silver coin, and the one who finds it in his portion is considered fortunate indeed. Norwegians bake a special rice pudding for the Yule dinner in which an almond is hidden, and the one to get the almond will be the first married!

Fish is popular in some of the European countries as a Christmas dish. In Sweden the biggest and finest fishes of the year are saved for Yule, blessed by the priests and prepared in the special way that only a Swedish housewife knows. At the Christmas feast it is served as *lut-fisk,* the main dish on the table. Other Scandinavian countries also serve fish at their feast, while Italians prefer eels for Christmas, and in Spain sea bream is eaten in accordance with a very old custom.

A salad dish that is served exclusively on Christmas Eve in Mexico has been named for the holy night—*Ensalada de la Noche Buena.* It is made from a mixture of many fruits and vegetables and garnished with gay-colored candies. The Ukrainian housewife has a big meal to prepare on Christmas Eve, for according to tradition, she must have twelve different kinds of food on the table at the Holy Supper. One of these is the traditional *kutia,* partaken of by every member of the family when prayers are said and wishes expressed for the coming year. Then the housewife dashes some of the *kutia* from a spoon into every corner of the house, saying: "May all evil fail to take to our sheep and cattle, as this wheat fails to take to the wall!"

Every good Serb eats roast pig on Christmas Day in honor of *Bozhitch,* an ancient sun god of pagan times who somehow became so closely identified with Christmas traditions that his name in the Serbian language now means Christmas.

In Finland, the week before Christmas finds the mother of the house pounding oats for the St. Stephen's Day porridge, the customary dish to eat there on Christmas Day, which is also celebrated in that country as the Eve of St. Stephen's.

Christmas dinner for the Shakers, a small communitarian sect in the eastern part of the United States, stands out from all other meals of the year, for it is the only time the men and women sit down to a meal together. With the men seated at one side of the long table and the women at the other, the meal is eaten in perfect silence. However, after the Christmas repast, all stand at their places and go through the ceremonious "shaking" dance that has given these people their name. This is probably the most unusual Christmas feast in our country.

While speaking of Christmas foods we certainly must not neglect the American roast turkey, the eating of which has become so truly an American custom. Other countries, too, have discovered this delicious fowl introduced to the Pilgrim Fathers three hundred years ago by the Indians. In Mexico it is prepared with *tortillas* and fried peppers.

Christmas is celebrated in the Orient in many homes and in all of the big cities. Santa Claus is known by the Japanese children as *Hoteiosho*—a god who is always pictured as carrying a pack, and is said to have eyes in the back of his head so he can see the children at all times. In many places there are community trees trimmed with lights and tinsel. The Christmas trees in the missionary compounds of India would certainly surprise American children, for very often they are banana trees with bananas still growing upon them and trimmings interlacing the fruit!

The custom of decorating our houses with evergreens at Christmas comes from the Romans. It was considered good luck to exchange branches of green on the Kalends of January, and gradually the custom was adopted by those who observed Christmas. With the Druids, those ancient pagans, mistletoe was a token of good luck, possibly because they believed it had great curative powers. Christmas decorations were at first used only in the churches.

Holly and Ivy, Box and Bay,
Put in the church on Christmas Day,

an old rhyme said.

Christmas trees are thought to have been introduced to Americans by Hessian Germans sent here by the English to fight in the American Revolution. The custom became so popular, much later, that the growing of Christmas trees has now become a thriving industry. The trees are grown in controlled forests or on Christmas tree farms, most of them privately owned. Though millions of trees are cut each year, supplies increase because of the scientific way they

210

are grown. Western and midwestern states harvest the largest crops. Montana alone produces at least three million trees annually.

Christmas tree companies contract with the growers for distribution of the trees. Wholesalers sell to the retailer, who is the Christmas tree seller on the local sidewalk or vacant lot. Thus the tree reaches the American living room and graces the holiday festivities.

Today the Finnish people "pave the way" for the Christ Child by cutting and piling up great pine boughs, making a huge green carpet from the top of a hill down to the heart of the village. Then everyone lights "luck chips"—pinewood tapers that have been buried in the snow for three days. Good luck is supposed to come to those whose tapers burn well.

The Greek Orthodox Church calls Christmas the Feast of Lights. As the Light of the World, Christ is represented in every land by the numerous lights of Christmas: candles, tapers, lights on the Christmas tree, and electric stars reminiscent of the Christmas star that shone down on the shepherds and their flocks on that first Holy Night long ago. In Ireland a tall candle is kept burning in the window all night to light the Christ Child on His way. A beautiful custom of the Moravian Church in America is the traditional "lovefeast," a candle service held on Christmas Eve especially for the children. Everyone in the congregation is given a tiny, lighted beeswax candle in commemoration of the coming of Christ, the coming of Light into the world. A child soloist leads the antiphonal musical part of this impressive service.

In Italy, Spain, Mexico, and other countries where the Yuletide season comes during the warm season, flowers are used for Christmas decoration instead of evergreens. In Mexico the *Noche Buena,* a beautiful scarlet plant, is in full bloom and used profusely for decorating the homes and churches; while in Australia a red and green Christmas Bush and the delicate Christmas Bell are in luxuriant growth.

Although we here in America observe only Christmas Eve and Christmas Day, the holiday in many countries lasts much longer. We have seen how the Mexicans observe two full weeks, and the same is true in Spain. In Holland and Belgium St. Nicholas comes December 6 to distribute gifts to the children. Sweden begins to celebrate on December 13, which is St. Lucia's Day, and in Norway the Yule begins on St. Thomas's Day, December 21, and lasts until New Year's. In Ireland, the days from St. Stephen's Eve (December 25) until Twelfth Night are kept as holidays with little or no work done, while mummers sing their carols to remind people that this is the blessed Christmas time.

Christmas customs in the United States vary according to the sections, depending upon the origin of the people who have settled there. In the valleys of Pennsylvania where the Pennsylvania Dutch have settled, there are traces of

German and Swiss customs. Out in the Middle West, particularly in Minnesota and Wisconsin, the Scandinavians have influenced Christmas observances. But there are some customs that are distinctly American. The southern states, for example, have a practice of shooting off fireworks on Christmas. Children receive gifts of sparklers, fountains, and other pretty fireworks in their stockings to be put off Christmas night. Unique, too, is the custom all over the country, of trimming trees and shrubbery on the lawn with bright electric lights.

Our Santa Claus is distinctly an American personality. In other countries he is pictured as a tall, dignified saint robed in all the official vestments of a bishop, while our patron saint of children is a fat, jolly, countrified-looking gentleman defying all the convention of the former Bishop of Myra in his make-up! This purely American type of Santa is due to a great extent to a famous poem written in 1822. Dr. Clement Moore wrote "The Night Before Christmas" (originally entitled "A Visit from St. Nicholas") for his own children, but when it appeared in print, first in a newspaper and later in a collection of his poetry, it was instantly taken to the hearts of American children everywhere. This jolly St. Nick of reindeer and sleigh and a pack full of toys has brought joy to millions of boys and girls and has been to them for many years the only true Santa Claus. With his description as expressed in the famous poem we close this story of Christmas.

He was dressed all in fur from his head to his foot,
And his clothes were all tarnished with ashes and soot;
A bundle of toys he had flung on his back,
And he looked like a pedlar just opening his pack.

His eyes—how they twinkled! his dimples how merry!
His cheeks were like roses, his nose like a cherry!
His droll little mouth was drawn up like a bow,
And the beard on his chin was as white as the snow;
The stump of a pipe he held tight in his teeth,
And the smoke it encircled his head like a wreath;
He had a broad face and a little round belly,
That shook when he laughed like a bowl full of jelly.

He was chubby and plump, a right jolly old elf,
And I laughed when I saw him, in spite of myself;
A wink of his eye and a twist of his head
Soon gave me to know I had nothing to dread.

He spoke not a word, but went straight to his work,
And filled all the stockings; then turned with a jerk,
And laying his finger aside of his nose,
And giving a nod, up the chimney he rose;

He sprang to his sleigh, to his team gave a whistle,
And away they all flew like the down of a thistle.
But I heard him exclaim, ere he drove out of sight,
HAPPY CHRISTMAS TO ALL AND TO ALL
A GOOD NIGHT!

Other Special Days

American Indian Day

FOURTH FRIDAY IN SEPTEMBER

Observed by Arizona, California, Illinois, Minnesota, Montana, New Mexico, New York, South Dakota, Washington, and Wisconsin. First celebrated by New York May 13, 1916, it was established for the purpose of recognizing and honoring the American Indian and improving his condition. The President of the American Indian Association, Sherman Coolidge, an Arapahoe Indian, asked that this day be observed "as one set apart as a memorial to the red race of America and to a wise consideration of its future, . . . as a part of the American people." Many changes have taken place in the condition of the American Indian as a result of the Indian Reorganization Act of June 18, 1934.

In 1936 a secret vote was taken in the tribes in which the Indians were asked to decide whether or not they wished to continue with the tribal form of government. The result was that 195 tribes voted to continue with it; 77 tribes rejected it. The old laws by which Indians were given lands by the government and then allowed to sell them were abolished. Indian tribal lands may not be sold. In 1948 franchise rights were granted to Indians. There have been marked improvements in the educational system with an endeavor to give the American Indian vocational training, thereby making him self-supporting.

In 1961, Secretary of the Interior Stewart Udall announced an intensive program to develop the Indian Reservations' natural resources, at the same time advancing opportunities for education. A number of new manufacturing plants were established to provide job opportunities for the Indians.

Armed Forces Day

THIRD SATURDAY IN MAY

Until 1949 the United States observed three separate "days" in recognition of three branches of the military: Army Day, April 6; Navy Day, October 27; Air Force Day, the second Saturday in September. Mostly through the influence of Secretary of Defense James V. Forrestal, all branches of the Armed Services were united into one Department of Defense. By proclamation of President Harry S. Truman, the first Armed Forces Day was celebrated on the third Saturday in May, 1950. That date is proclaimed annually by the President. Special programs for the day are held by the Army, Navy, and Air Force.

Bird Day

USUALLY SECOND WEEK IN APRIL

Often observed with Arbor Day, it was first celebrated in 1894 by the schools of Oil City, Pennsylvania. Started by the National Association of Audubon Societies for the Protection of Wild Birds and Animals, its observance is sponsored by the United States Department of Agriculture.

Boy Scout Day

FEBRUARY 8

This is the anniversary of the founding of the Boy Scouts of America in 1910, and is the first day of Boy Scout Week, observed by Scouts all over the United States and its possessions.

Bunker Hill Day

JUNE 17

Commemorates the Battle of Bunker Hill, at Bunker Hill, Boston, Massachusetts, on June 17, 1775. Although this battle was lost to the British, it was a "moral victory" giving the colonists confidence, after having seen the British retreat twice. At the site of the battle where Joseph Warren, American patriot, was killed stands the Bunker Hill Monument, the cornerstone of which was laid by Lafayette in

1825. It was at that ceremony that Daniel Webster made one of the greatest orations of his career. The day is a holiday in Boston and in Suffolk County, Massachusetts.

Candlemas

FEBRUARY 2

February 2 is popularly known in America as Groundhog Day, but it is also, and more traditionally, Candlemas. The name Candlemas comes from the custom of the blessing of candles by the clergy and their distribution to members of the congregation, one of the most beautiful of all church ceremonies. In the Roman Catholic Church Candlemas is celebrated as the Purification of the Virgin. This festival is also observed in the Orthodox Catholic Church and the Protestant Episcopal Church. At its beginning, in Jerusalem, the day was known simply as the fortieth day after Epiphany, but in the fourth century the date was changed to February 2. Beeswax candles are blessed, sprinkled and incensed, then distributed, and while the choir sings the antiphon *"Adorna thalamum tuum, Sion,"* the clergy and the laity carry the lighted candles in a solemn march through the church. According to the *Catholic Encyclopedia,* "The solemn procession represents the entry of Christ, who is the Light of the World, into the Temple of Jerusalem."

Candlemas has been for centuries a popular day for weather prognostications, probably originating in the pre-Christian era. An old rhyme said:

If Candlemas day be dry and fair,
The half o' winter's to come and mair;
If Candlemas day be wet and foul,
The half o' winter's gone at Yule.

This was not the only superstition regarding the day. It was considered ill luck to permit the Christmas greens to remain in the house after Candlemas.

The snowdrop is known in England as the Candlemas or Purification flower. In Scotland on Candlemas there is a long-standing custom whereby the children give small gifts of money to their teachers. In Mexico, people think of Candlemas as the time when Christmas celebrations are brought to an end, for Christmas is probably celebrated there more extensively than in any other nation of the world.

Ground-hog Day originated with the Germans. The idea was brought to America by settlers who held the belief that the badger was a weather prognosticator! In the eastern states, where there are no badgers, it is the ground hog who sees his shadow, or doesn't see it, according to the condition of the weather on February 2. If Mr. Ground Hog finds bright skies when he comes out of his hole and sees his shadow, he withdraws once more to remain for another six weeks, thus retarding spring for that long! On the other hand, if the sky is overcast and the weather is dull throughout the day, Mr. Ground Hog walks abroad and the sign is portentous! Spring is on its way. In some rural sections this superstition has become so deep-rooted that farmers plan

their crops accordingly. In Lancaster County, where the Pennsylvania German farmers hold to this belief of their forefathers, there is an organization called the Slumbering Ground-hog Lodge. A group of farmers from this famous farming center goes through the ritual every year on the second of February of discovering what the ground hog does. Depending upon that small animal and his habits, and the sun, they prognosticate the weather of the next six weeks just as their forefathers did many years before them.

Citizenship Day

SEPTEMBER 17

Replaced Constitution Day (same date), and I Am an American Day (third Sunday in May). The latter was created by Congress in 1940 for the purpose of honoring new citizens of the United States who had reached voting age or became eligible to vote through naturalization. It was celebrated the third Sunday in May. In February, 1952, it was changed by an act of Congress to Citizenship Day, with the date of celebration set for September 17, the anniversary of the signing of the United States Constitution, September 17, 1787.

Election Day, General

FIRST TUESDAY AFTER THE FIRST MONDAY IN NOVEMBER

By an act of Congress in 1845 this day was set for the election of the President and Vice-President of the United States. In 1872 a law was passed making the date also the time for the election of Congressmen. State elections are held at the same time in all but the State of Maine, where they are held in September. General Election Day is a legal holiday in thirty-seven states.

Father's Day

THIRD SUNDAY IN JUNE

First celebrated June 19, 1910, the day was originated by Mrs. John Bruce Dodd and sponsored by the Ministerial Association of Washington, D.C. Since 1935, a national Father's Day Committee in New York City has chosen America's "Father of the Year."

Fire Prevention Day

OCTOBER 9

This date was chosen because the Chicago Fire was on October 8 and 9 in 1871. Since 1911 the first week of October has been observed as Fire Prevention Week.

Forefathers' Day

DECEMBER 22

Celebrated by New England Societies everywhere as an anniversary of the landing of the Pilgrims at Plymouth Rock in 1620; observed since 1769.

Inauguration Day

JANUARY 20

Formerly March 4 and changed in 1933 to the present date, it is held every fourth year to inaugurate the President and Vice-President of the United States in the nation's capital. It is a legal holiday in Washington, D.C.

Jackson Day

JANUARY 8

Legal in Louisiana. Celebrated by Democrats all over the United States with Jackson Day dinners. The date commemorates Jackson's victory at New Orleans, January 8, 1815.

Jefferson Davis Day

JUNE 3

Observed by the southern states. Jefferson Davis, American statesman, was born June 3, 1808; was President of the Confederacy during the Civil War; died 1889.

Jefferson's Birthday

APRIL 13

The birthday of Thomas Jefferson is a legal holiday in Alabama, Missouri, and Virginia. It is a memorial day in Nebraska.

Labor Day

FIRST MONDAY IN SEPTEMBER

This legal holiday observed to honor Labor was inaugurated by the Knights of Labor, an organization founded in Philadelphia in 1869. In 1887 Colorado named May 1 as Labor Day, and several other states followed suit, but in 1894 the date was changed permanently to the first Monday in September, and the day became a national holiday. Many countries, however, do observe Labor Day on May 1, with Labor Union parades and mass meetings. In the Soviet Union, this is a national holiday. In Yugoslavia it is known as Workers' Day. In Australia it is celebrated as Eight-Hour Day in honor of the shorter working day adopted there some years ago.

In the United States it is considered a day of rest and recreation and is generally the end of the vacation season. Holiday traffic is very heavy over the Labor Day weekend, often resulting in a terrible toll of traffic deaths. Classes in most public schools begin the day after Labor Day.

Lee's Birthday

JANUARY 19

A legal holiday in most southern states. Robert Edward Lee, born January 19, 1807, was a distinguished soldier before the Civil War. Asked by Lincoln to take command of the U.S. Army, he refused, saying that he could not fight against his mother state of Virginia. He took command of the Confederate Army, 1861–65; died 1870. Lee is considered to have been one of the greatest generals the world has ever known.

Mardi Gras

(See also *Shrove Tuesday*)

THE DAY BEFORE LENT BEGINS

Mardi gras carnivals are held in New Orleans, Louisiana, and several other southern cities. The most famous, in New Orleans, has been held since 1766, when it was intro-

duced by French settlers. Celebrated for a week, with the largest parades and balls on Shrove Tuesday, it attracts tourists from all over this country, Mexico, and Canada. The week's events are sponsored by secret clubs or krewes, the largest of which are Rex and Comus Krewes. A holiday air reigns over the carnival city, which throngs with great crowds in gayest mood.

National Freedom Day

FEBRUARY 1

This day marks the anniversary of the signing by President Abraham Lincoln of an amendment to the Constitution to abolish slavery, on February 1, 1865. The Emancipation Proclamation, signed by Lincoln, January 1, 1863, had applied only to slaves held in territories that were in rebellion against the United States. This important amendment of 1865 freed also all the slaves in the North.

National Freedom Day was authorized by Congress in 1948. It is observed annually by proclamation.

National Maritime Day

MAY 22

This date was chosen in commemoration of the sailing from Savannah, Georgia, on May 22, 1819, of the *Savannah,* the first successful steam-propelled boat to cross the ocean. The day was set by President Franklin D. Roosevelt in 1935 when he declared "That May 22 of each year shall hereafter be designated and known as National Maritime Day, and the President is authorized and requested annually to issue a proclamation calling upon the people of the United States to observe such National Maritime Day by displaying the flag at their homes or other suitable places and Government officials to display the flag on all Government buildings on May 22 of each year."

Patriots' Day

APRIL 19

A legal holiday in Massachusetts and Maine, commemorating the Battles of Lexington and Concord on April 19, 1775.

Pioneer Days

DATES DIFFER IN DIFFERENT STATES

Idaho celebrates Pioneer Day on June 15 as a legal holiday in honor of the first settlement at Franklin, Idaho. It is observed in Utah on July 24, the anniversary of Brigham Young's first sighting of the spot that became Salt Lake City. Pioneer Days are held annually during the first week of July in Landers, Wyoming, with a rodeo, parades, and a pageant depicting life in the early days.

Roosevelt's Birthday

JANUARY 30

Franklin Delano Roosevelt, thirty-second President of the United States, was born January 30, 1882. In the midst of an active political life he became stricken with poliomyelitis, a crippling disease that took a heavy toll annually in the United States, especially among children. In spite of his handicap from the disease, Mr. Roosevelt became Governor of New York and then President of the United States. Throughout his lifetime, one of his greatest interests was in helping to control polio and rehabilitate those who were its victims. After he became President, a move was started to help with the work at Warm Springs, Georgia, where he himself had been a patient. His birthday, January 30, was the date chosen to hold a drive for funds.

The first celebration of Roosevelt's Birthday for this purpose was held in 1934 when nearly a million dollars was raised at "Birthday Balls" held throughout the nation.

In 1938, the National Foundation for Infantile Paralysis was incorporated. President Roosevelt announced that its aims were "to lead, direct and unify" the war on polio. From that time, the movement was shared by people all over the United States. Benefits from the drives (no longer going to Warm Springs) were divided between the National Foundation and the communities where the funds were raised. Contributions came from everyone through the nationwide March of Dimes plan of giving. The money raised year after year in this effort resulted in extensive research into the causes and cure of polio. The two greatest contributions from grants made by the March of Dimes were the anti-polio "killed-virus" vaccine developed in 1955 by Dr. Jonas E. Salk, and the "live-virus" vaccine developed by Dr. Albert B. Sabin in 1959. These and other accomplishments of the National Foundation have almost removed the scourge of polio from the list of diseases of mankind. The work of the Foundation continues through the unique and wonderful manner of celebrating a birthday.

Roosevelt's Birthday is a legal holiday in Kentucky. It is celebrated by every state, territory, and possession of the United States.

Shrove Tuesday
(See also *Mardi gras*)
TUESDAY BEFORE LENT

Observed as Mardi gras in Alabama, some cities in Florida, and Louisiana. Where Germans have settled, it is known as *Fastnacht,* and the people celebrate it by eating *fastnachts,* or doughnuts. Often it is called Pancake Day because of a popular custom of eating pancakes on this day.

United Nations Day
OCTOBER 24

This is the anniversary of the day in 1945 that the United Nations was officially established at a meeting in San Francisco. Two years later, on October 31, 1947, the General Assembly declared that United Nations Day should be observed each year on October 24. The day is proclaimed annually by the President of the United States and is also observed by most members of the United Nations. The UN flag is raised over public buildings in member countries; programs are held in many different languages; post-office departments cancel letters on that day with the words

228

"United Nations Day" in their own language. Thus, United Nations Day is a special day that is celebrated all around the world.

Whitsunday

SEVENTH SUNDAY AFTER EASTER

Commemorating the day when the Holy Ghost descended upon the Disciples, this day is observed by all Christian churches in countries throughout the world. The name comes from the white garb worn by those who are baptized on that day. There is an old saying that a wish made exactly at sunrise on Whitsunday will come true.

Whitmonday is a legal holiday in the Virgin Islands.

Jewish Holidays and Fast Days

New Year—TISHRI 1.
Fast of Guedaliah—TISHRI 3.
Day of Atonement—TISHRI 10.
Tabernacles, First Day—TISHRI 15.
Tabernacles, Eighth Day—TISHRI 22.
Rejoicing of the Law—TISHRI 23.
Channukah—KISLEV 25.
Fast of Tebet—TEBET 10.
Purim—ADAR 14.
Passover, First Day—NISAN 15.
Passover, Seventh Day—NISAN 21.
Passover, Last Day—NISAN 22.

Shabouth, Feast of Weeks—SIVAN 6.
Fast of Tammuz—TAMMUZ 17.
Fast of Abh—ABH 9.

Principal Festivals of the Orthodox Catholic Church

Resurrection, Ascension, Pentecost, Birth of the Virgin Mary, Elevation of the Cross, Entrance of the Virgin Mary into the Temple, Christmas, Epiphany, Presentation, Annunciation, Transfiguration, Dormition.

Principal Festivals of the Roman Catholic Church

Easter, Epiphany, Whitsunday, Ascension, Corpus Christi, The Sacred Heart, Assumption, Immaculate Conception, St. John the Baptist, St. Joseph, SS. Peter and Paul, All Saints', Christmas.

Story of the Calendar

For thousands of years, ever since the dawn of civilization, men have employed some method of measuring time. Time has always been an important element in the lives of men of all ages and races, and so, for convenience's sake, the calendar was invented. The word calendar comes from the Roman *kalends* meaning the first of the month, but calendars were in use for many centuries before the Roman Empire. In the time of the Ancient Egyptians the length of a solar year was determined by observing the shadows cast by those ageless wonders, the pyramids. And even before the beginning of actual recorded history we know there must have been various ways of counting the succession of days and months and years—this "Checker-board of Nights and Days," as Omar Khayyam so appropriately expressed it nearly a thousand years ago.

Counting nights instead of days was a custom of the early Teutonic peoples. From this custom has come the term fortnight, meaning fourteen nights. Their calendar included no months and only three seasons, for autumn was omitted entirely in their division of the year. Instead of days they used tides as a measure—sixty tides to a month. About one hundred years before the time of Christ, they accepted the Roman, or pre-Julian, Calendar.

The first Roman calendar that we know anything about, supposed to have been created by Numa Pompilius in the seventh century B.C., usually contained about 304 days. In order to bring their time up to the correct solar year, an extra month was added every now and then by the priests to the tenth month, for ten months with weeks consisting of eight days each comprised this old calendar. About three hundred years before the time of the Cæsars, this calendar was amended by Cnæus Flavius. However, in Cicero's time it was inaccurate by six weeks, and in Julius Cæsar's time by two months! No wonder, then, that Cæsar found it to be unsatisfactory. It was he who set about making real reforms, giving us the basis of the calendar we use today.

By Cæsar's reckoning there were 365¼ days in the solar year, so he arranged to have an extra day every four years to take care of this odd six hours a year. The extra day was added by observing February the 24 *twice* in Leap Year.

But in order to bring the calendar up to date with the sun
he added two months to the year we now refer to as 46 B.C.,
inserting them beween the months of November and December. The year of the new calendar's adoption therefore
was the longest year on record; it contained 445 days! However, from the time the new Julian Calendar really went
into effect until the year 1582, no changes were made and
it worked remarkably well, considering the inefficiency of
previous calendars.

At the time Julius Cæsar began his calendar reforms there were only 355 days in the year. To these he added ten more in this wise: two at the end of January, August, and December; one at the end of April, June, July, and September. Have you ever wondered why there are thirty-one days in both July and August, the only two long months that come together, and why February is so short? Legend has it that a day was taken from February and added to August, to make it contain as many days as July, so that the month named for Augustus Cæsar should not seem inferior to the month named for Julius.

With the irregularity of the length of our months, it is fortunate that someone made up a verse as a reminder of the number of days contained in each.

Thirty days hath September,
April, June, and November,
All the rest have thirty-one,
Except February alone
Which has twenty-eight and one more
Added every year in four.

With the exception of the month of *Quintilis,* which became July, and the month *Sextilis,* now August, the names of the months remained as they had been, as follows:

March – named for Mars, Roman god of war.
April – from the Latin "aperio"—to open.
May – uncertainty as to whether from the little-known goddess Maia, or the word "maior"—increasing.

June – probably from Juno, though historians differ on this.

July – for Julius Cæsar.

August – for Augustus Cæsar.

September – seventh month (in the Roman calendar).

October – eighth month.

November – ninth month.

December – tenth month.

January – from the ancient Roman god of beginnings.

February – from Latin word "februum"—an instrument of purification.

Each month in the Roman Calendar had three important days—the calends or first of the month, the nones or fifth, and the ides or thirteenth. But to these there were exceptions as the verse explains.

March, July, October, May
Make Nones the seventh, Ides the fifteenth day.

Because of the fact that Julius Cæsar was slain on the ides of March, which came on the fifteenth day, and probably also because of the familiar quotation from Shakespeare's *Julius Caesar,* "Beware the ides of March," we are inclined to think of the ides as having been the fifteenth in every Roman month, instead of the exception.

The Roman week contained eight days, with seven working days ending in a big market day called the *nundina.* Originally Jewish, the seven-day week was not adopted in Rome until after the introduction of Christianity. Even

then, after a time, the people went back again to the eight-
day week. It was not until the Gregorian Calendar was
adopted that the seven-day week came to stay.

In studying the names of the days of the week we can
see that several languages and peoples influenced their naming, and that the origin of their names is distinctly pagan.
Because of their pagan origin, the days of the week and the
months are numbered instead of named by the Society of
Friends.

Sunday comes from *sunnandaeg,* Anglo-Saxon for sun
day. Likewise Monday is derived from moon day, *monan-
daeg.* Tuesday is for Tyr, Norse god of war, or, in the
Anglo-Saxon, *Tiwesdaeg.* Wednesday is *Wodnes daeg* for
Woden the high god of the Teutons, Thursday for the
Norse god of thunder, Thor. Friday was named for Thor's
wife, Freya. Saturday gets its name from the Roman god of
the harvest, Saturn, which in Anglo-Saxon is *Saeterdaeg.*

The custom of dating the years of the Christian era from
the year of Christ's birth as A.D.—*Anno Domini* (in the
year of our Lord) and designating the years before Christ
as B.C.—was conceived by a churchman of the sixth century,
Abbott Dionysius Exigus, by name. But somewhere, somehow, an error was made in the reckoning, and historians
believe that Jesus was really born some time between the
years 9 and 7 B.C. The exact date will never be known. Likewise the day and the month are not known exactly. For
many years at the beginning of the Christian era, unsuccess-
ful attempts were made to place both November 17 and

March 28 as the time of His birth. In the year A.D. 354 the
Roman Bishop Liberius began to celebrate Christ's birthday
on December 25, and that date has been kept ever since.

Although the calendar as Julius Cæsar had made it was
very nearly accurate, and is used to this day with some few
exceptions, that slight inaccuracy threw it off after several
hundred years. When the year 1582 rolled around, the
calendar was ten days behind the sun and Pope Gregory
decided to do something about it. So he dropped the ten

237

days! Julius Cæsar had reckoned 365¼ days to a year, but the year actually contains something less than he had figured; to be exact, the earth goes round the sun in 365 days, 5 hours, 48 minutes and 46 seconds. With the passing of centuries this inaccuracy had amounted to a difference more serious than the Roman emperor could have foreseen. After some calculations, Pope Gregory decided that a leap year dropped every now and then from the calendar would correct the difficulty. His figuring resulted in this conclusion: that every year divisible by 4 should be a leap year *except* when it was divisible by 100. But he made an exception to that rule, too, deciding that those years that are divisible by 400 should *be* a leap year, whether or no! In other words, the year 1600 was a leap year; the years 1700, 1800, 1900 were not. But the year 2000 will be a leap year because it is divisible by 400. In this way, and still observing the rule of "every year in four," the Gregorian Calendar has been called correct except for an additional 26 seconds every year! But since these additional seconds cannot total a full day until 3323 years have passed, there is little to worry about in the Gregorian Calendar as far as inaccuracies are concerned.

Although Pope Gregory's new calendar was accepted by Rome and made lawful in an act dated March 1, 1582, it was not until 1752 that Great Britain finally adopted it, at which time eleven days had to be dropped. In that year the dates in England went like this—September 1, 2, 14, 15, etc. Anyone whose birthday fell on a date between the second and fourteenth of September had to wait until the following year to celebrate it! But with the adoption of the Gregorian Calendar, the calendars of Great Britain were in line with those of most of the European countries that had been using the Gregorian for years. Scotland, for instance, had adopted it in 1600. Today the Gregorian is the national calendar of most countries of the civilized world. However, some people still use the Julian in reckoning their holidays. And for their church festivals various ancient calendars are still adhered to.

The Aztec Indians of Mexico had a solar calendar that was always shown in the form of a circle to depict the sun. Their year consisted of 18 months of 20 days each. To round out a total of 365 days, five days were added at the end of the year. The Aztecs believed that these days were unlucky.

Probably the oldest calendar still in use is the Hindu one, which was in existence at least five centuries before the birth of Christ, and is still used in many parts of India today.

It is interesting to know that there is still in common use a calendar that has been the same for nearly six thousand years. The ancient Hebrew Calendar of Biblical times is the same one that is used by Orthodox Jews today. Because it is based on a lunar year, there is a difference of more than eleven days between it and the calendar based on the solar year. In order to "catch up" with the sun's year the Hebrew Calendar adds a month, Adar Sheni, seven times in every nineteen years. The inaccuracy lies in the fact that twelve moons (a lunar year) do not quite make a solar year. The flexibility of the Hebrew Calendar makes the feasts and holidays come at different times every year on the modern calendar. The Jewish festivals are the oldest on record. Many of them are symbolic of the pastoral life led by the Hebrews in ancient times. To study Jewish holidays and their origin is to recognize the historic tradition of the Jewish people. Most important of all the holidays is *Yom Kippur*. The ten days between *Rosh Hashana* and *Yom Kippur* are known as the Days of Penitence. Other important festivals are the *Pesach* or Passover, coming about the time of our Easter and commemorating the exodus of the Children of Israel from the land of Egypt; also *Shabouth* the Feast of Weeks, and *Succoth* the Feast of Tabernacles.

The Moslem Calendar begins its year in December. Adopted in the year A.D. 622, it was put into effect by the great prophet Mohammed, founder of Islam. Although it is used today by the people of that faith, most Moslems use the Gregorian Calendar in their secular life.

For a short time in France a different calendar was tried out but found unsatisfactory. Adopted October 5, 1793, after the French Revolution, it was abolished on December 31, 1805, when the Gregorian Calendar was once more established. Known as the Republican and also the Revolutionary Calendar, it had twelve months of thirty days each, with five or six days added at the end of the year to make it agree with the solar year—not a very convenient arrangement.

A French philosopher, Auguste Comte, planned a thirteenth-month calendar in the early nineteenth century. It was never considered seriously because it was so drastically different from the traditional, but it may have influenced other reforms. Comte's calendar had thirteen months four weeks long, each week beginning with Sunday, and a "Year Day" between the end of December and the first of January to round out the 365 days.

Since 1923 there have been serious movements toward instituting a new calendar that could be used by all the countries of the world. A Calendar Council of the League of Nations worked for years on calendar reforms, and it is said that more than two hundred proposals were made. One of these was a "World Calendar" that was approved by seventeen nations in the Council. It was proposed by the World Calendar Association headed by Miss Elisabeth Achelis, who worked for many years toward its adoption. This calendar was composed of twelve months divided into equal quarters of three months each. The first month of each quarter would contain 31 days; the other two, 30 days each. The 365th day would be known as World's Day; a leap-year day, a world holiday, would come every fourth year between June and July. One of the advantages over the present calendar would be the uniform length of each quarter, making statistical comparisons much easier.

A "Universal Calendar," planned by Professor Walter F. Rothé, was introduced to the United Nations in 1956. Its sponsors, the Universal Calendar Society, have called it "an International Perpetual Calendar impartial to all nations,

241

races and religions with the closest possible astronomical regularity." It is composed of 13 equal months of 20 days each, each week and each month to begin on Monday; each week and each month to end on Sunday. The extra month (seventh month on this calendar) would be Solarius. The 365th day of the year would be called Earth-Orbit Day, while a leap-year day would be placed between the two equal halves of the year on every fourth year. Each quarter would consist of 91 days. With the uniform length of weeks, months, and quarters, business statistics would be greatly simplified. It has been pointed out by its sponsors that the Universal Calendar, because it is based on scientific calculations, is as precise as the clock by which we count the hours of the day.

Whether or not a new calendar is adopted depends upon a great many factors. There are unquestionably many advantages from the standpoint of efficiency, convenience, and international unity. On the other hand, our present method of reckoning time, with only slight changes, is about two thousand years old, and custom dies hard. Involved in so drastic a change are tradition, custom, and even superstition. But the people of Cæsar's time got used to a new calendar, and the British finally surrendered their Julian Calendar, in spite of much bitter opposition, in favor of the Gregorian. If a new calendar is adopted within our time we will, undoubtedly, do as well as they in adjusting ourselves to the change.

Index

Index

Elizabeth Hough Sechrist

became interested in writing for children while she was a Children's Librarian in Bethlehem, Pennsylvania. Each year she was asked by boys and girls, teachers, and librarians for information on Christmas in other lands. Because of the lack of material, she began to collect and write on the subject herself, and the resulting book, *Christmas Everywhere,* has been popular in schools and libraries for many years.

After nine years' experience in Bethlehem and Pittsburgh libraries, Mrs. Sechrist gave up her work to devote her time to writing, editing, and lecturing on children's books—and, incidentally, to keeping house in York, Pennsylvania.

Author of eight books and co-author with her good friend Janette Woolsey of seven more, she claims the days are never long enough!